TOWER HAMLETS

91 000 001 609 18 9

KT-473-526

Anjum's INDIAN VEGETARIAN FEAST

Anjum Anand

Photography by Emma Lee

Quadrille PUBLISHING

TOWER HAMLETS
LIBRARIES

91000001609189

Bertrams	17/09/2012
641.563	£19.99
THISBO	TH12000811

To Adi and Mahi, with all my love... always.

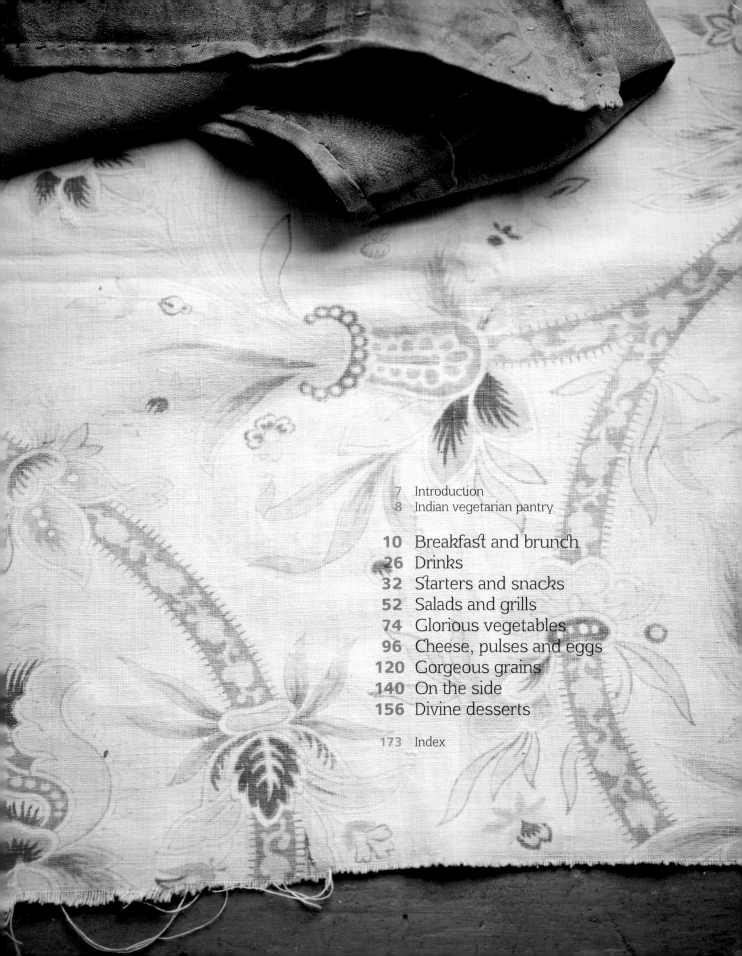

I was raised by a vegetarian mother. She had an arranged marriage, which makes you think she would have been introduced to a 'suitable' partner, but really my father couldn't have been more different from her when it came to food. His tastes were as gourmand as hers were restrained. He tells colourful stories about fishing with his brothers, taking their prize catch home and making a big pot of curry, but food never features in my mother's childhood tales. Once married, however, she started to cook the rich, meaty curries my father loved, and served them up as well as her simple but equally tasty vegetable and lentil dishes. I was brought up eating both.

In a funny twist of fate, I then married a vegetarian who comes from generations of vegetarians. So my children are vegetarian. As I have been married for nine years – and my husband doesn't cook – that's a lot of vegetarian meals. Like my mother, I have learned a new way to cook, creating new dishes and tinkering with flavours to keep my family well fed and enjoying their meals.

Luckily, my culinary heritage is replete with amazing vegetarian dishes, as two-thirds of India has followed a meat-free diet for thousands of years, either because the people can't afford meat on a regular basis, or because they believe that eating it is bad for the soul (in a country that believes in reincarnation, they aren't taking any chances). Either way, this has given them a lot of time to perfect the culinary uses of lentils, beans and dairy products into a vast spectrum of dishes. I have always said my desert island ingredient would be the humble Bengal gram (chana dal), a type of lentil. It can be made into a curry, stir-fried with spices into a protein-rich side dish, even used to make a dessert. It is also ground into flour and then made into bread, or batter for spiced pancakes or bhajis, or spiced and steamed savoury lentil cakes. Indians are alchemists of the vegetarian table, and can conjure thousands of uses from their beans or dairy products.

The recipes in this book have their feet firmly planted in India's amazing regional food, but also contain influences from my life and travels. Many of the dishes here are Indian classics, others are refreshed and revised meals that I love. There are also a few which are just hanging by a home-spun cotton thread to an Indian heritage, but are too delicious not to be included.

I have enjoyed writing this book more than any other; I've cooked with foods I hadn't tried before and experimented with new flavour combinations. I find the world of meat-free living bountiful, beautiful and a feast for so many of the senses. I hope you enjoy the food as much as I do.

Anjum.

Indian vegetarian pantry

Most of the ingredients necessary to whip up exciting, nourishing vegetarian food can be kept handy in your pantry. As long as you have the very basic fresh ingredients – such as onions, root ginger, garlic, tomatoes and yogurt – you should be able to whip up delicious meals without last-minute dashes to the shops. This is a really comprehensive list, so don't feel that you need to buy and store all of these in your kitchen, but do have a look through and see which make you feel hungry! The more varied your vegetarian diet the better, so be adventurous and seek out ingredients that you don't eat... yet.

PULSES

Obviously, these are a great source of protein, as well as key minerals. I store both dried and canned beans. I prefer the texture and flavour of dried beans, which need to be soaked overnight before cooking, but I also have cans of those beans I eat often, just in case of sudden cravings. I never buy canned lentils, as these do not need soaking. There are a whole panoply of lentils and they are your friends in the kitchen: they need little attention and minimal fuss to fashion into beautiful curries. Here are some of the bean and lentil varieties I use most often.

BEANS	LENTILS
Black-eyed beans	Bengal gram *(chana dal)*
Butterbeans	Black gram *(urad dal)*
Cannellini beans	Puy lentils
Chickpeas	Red lentils *(masoor dal)*
Kidney beans	Split black gram
	(dhuli hui ma dal)
	Split pigeon peas *(toor dal)*
	Yellow lentils *(mung dal)*

SPICES

Essential to the Indian diet; Indians are the alchemists of the spice rack. I recommend you increase your spice larder by one jar or packet a week, as these will really add a wow factor to your daily diet.

WHOLE	GROUND
Black cardamom pods	Asafoetida
Black peppercorns	Chaat masala
Brown mustard seeds	*(a store-bought blend of tangy*
Carom seeds	*spices, this is really useful)*
Cassia bark *(a hardier, less*	Chilli powder
sweet version of cinnamon)	Dried fenugreek leaves
Cloves	*(a great savoury flavour)*
Coriander seeds	Dried mint
Cumin seeds	*(adds lovely fragrance)*
Curry leaves *(ideally fresh;*	Mango powder
if dried or frozen, use with	*(gives a welcome sour note)*
a heavier hand)	Pomegranate powder *(with*
Dried red chillies	*an unusual, delicious tang)*
Fennel seeds	Turmeric
Fenugreek seeds	
Green cardamom pods	
Mace	
Nutmeg	
Panch phoran	
(a mix of five seeds)	

How to roast spices

Only roast whole spices. Place the spices in a moderately hot, dry frying pan and toast over a gentle heat. Shake the pan often so the spices brown evenly. (Do not use non-stick pans as the coating may smoke and this is thought to be toxic.) As the spices roast, they colour and become aromatic. Take them off the heat once they turn a few shades darker. (For the already dark spices, test by aroma instead.) Remove them from the pan or they will continue to brown and might burn. Roasted spices can be ground in a mortar and pestle, or a spice or coffee grinder kept for the purpose.

GRAINS

These don't have to be dull, in fact these days they are positively fashionable! Some can add protein to the diet.

Basmati rice, white and brown.
I use a lot of brown at home for family food.
Beaten rice *(poha)*.
This is cooked rice that has been dried, then flattened into a flake. It is fluffy and delicious and often made into a pilaf. Don't confuse this with the flaked raw rice that you can buy in some supermarkets.
Bulgar wheat, nutty and delicious.
Chapati flour *(atta)*, made from whole wheat berries.
Gram flour *(besan)*, made from chickpeas.
This has a lovely flavour and is high in protein.
Quinoa. Another high-protein grain that is really good as part of a vegetarians diet.
Semolina. A lovely, couscous-like grain that can be used in a batter to add crunch, or in a pilaf or dessert.

NUTS AND SEEDS

Nuts feature heavily in Indian food, giving texture or flavour, or working as thickening agents. I have also included in this book chia seeds, which are believed by many to be very healthy, especially good for vegetarians, and, once softened in liquid, have an interesting gelatinous texture. I have used them in this book in my kulfi recipe, but I often add some to my porridge or yogurt.

Almonds	Peanuts, roasted or raw
Cashews	Pistachios, roasted or raw
Coconut: milk, cream,	Poppy seeds
desiccated, and frozen	Sesame seeds
and grated	

How to make paneer

Paneer is an unsalted, crumbly white Indian cheese which is really easy to make.
Bring 2 litres of whole milk to a boil in a heavy-based pan; stir and scrape the base often to ensure the milk does not burn. Boil for five minutes, then add 250g live yogurt or the juice of 1 lemon (yogurt gives a softer paneer). Stir while it splits into curds and whey. Line a colander with a muslin cloth (or other clean cloth) and pour in the contents of the pan. Rinse with cold water. Tie the cloth into a sack, then tie this to the kitchen tap and allow to drain for 20 minutes. Next, place it on a thick board, still enclosed, and pat it out so it forms a 2.5cm-thick disc. Place a large weight on top (I use a saucepan filled with water) and put the board in the sink. The water will seep out. Leave until it solidifies; this will take 1–2 hours, more for a solid paneer, less for a softer texture. This recipe yields 250g of paneer. Keep, stored in water, in the fridge. Before cooking, soak in hot water for five to 10 minutes to soften.

NOTES ON...

...ROOT GINGER In many recipes I read, ginger is measured by length, but I find this an unreliable way to measure the rhizome, as the thickness can vary so much. I measure it in grams, or sometimes teaspoons, to get just the right amount of ginger flavour every time.

...CHILLIES The heat varies from batch to batch, and this extends to chilli powder, so always add sparingly. You can always add extra chilli powder at the end of cooking for more heat, if you want it.

...DOUBLING RECIPES As a general rule you can double all the recipes in this book, but you have to be careful about the amount of spices you use. Only add another 50 per cent of the whole spices used, to double a recipe. (The exception to this rule is cumin seeds; you should double the amount of these.)

BREAKFAST AND BRUNCH

A lovely weekend breakfast dish; easy but really special. Brioche is the best bread to use in my opinion, as the resulting toast is both buttery and soft on the inside and lightly crisp on the outside, but your everyday loaf of bread would be just fine, too. Desiccated coconut is one of my storecupboard staples and here it adds a lovely texture as well as its sun-drenched, coastal flavour. If I am making this for guests at a weekend brunch, I add fresh seasonal soft fruit on the side as well as a little Greek yogurt and a handful of Jaggery Caramelised Walnuts (see below).

Coconut French toast

Whisk together the eggs, milk and sugar. Spread the desiccated coconut on a small plate.

Heat the oil and butter in a large non-stick frying pan over a medium flame. Dip one slice of bread in the batter for about 30–40 seconds, pressing lightly to help the bread absorb the custard. Transfer to the plate of desiccated coconut and press gently, turning to coat both sides. Place straight in the hot pan, then repeat with the other slices.

Cook over a moderate flame for about two minutes, or until golden, then carefully flip and brown the other side. Serve hot from the pan, or keep warm while you cook the rest. Offer maple syrup on the table for those who want extra sweetness.

SERVES 4

2 large eggs
200ml whole milk
3 tbsp sugar (use only 2 tbsp if you are going
    to serve these with syrup)
6 good tbsp desiccated coconut
2 tbsp vegetable oil
couple of knobs of unsalted butter
4 slices of brioche, or everyday bread
natural maple syrup, to serve (optional)

Jaggery caramelised walnuts
MAKES A SMALL BATCH

I love these scattered over sweet breakfasts, or they make a great snack when I want something sweet but healthy. Jaggery is a completely unrefined sugar, sold in blocks and renowned for its healthy properties. It is full of iron and other minerals and believed to keep your lungs clean. The best quality is dark and hard, but larger supermarkets sell a softer jaggery which also works here.

Take 80g of jaggery and chop or pound it into smallish pieces. Place in a frying pan and cook over a medium-low flame, stirring often, until it melts and starts to get more glassy and less cloudy; this only takes a few minutes. Stir in 80g of walnuts, stir to coat well and cook for another minute. Pour out on to a sheet of baking parchment, or an oiled plate, and separate the walnuts. You have to work quickly as the jaggery will start to harden. (If so, return to the pan and heat a little to melt it again.) Allow to cool and harden. Store in an airtight container.

Bananas are one of Kerala's most prolific fruits and are used in everything. In Kerala at breakfast time, they might be simply sliced on top of rice pancakes, or steamed in batter in a banana leaf, or mixed with grated coconut and cashews and used to fill a pancake. My own version definitely uses western artistic licence, as the bananas are mashed into a quick and easy American-inspired fluffy pancake. I add cumin seeds to the batter, but you can leave them out if you prefer.

Keralan-inspired banana pancakes with peanut butter

Heat the rounded tbsp of butter in a small saucepan over a gentle heat until it is lightly browned and smells nutty, then set aside.

Mix together the flour, salt, sugar, baking powder and cumin seeds. In a separate bowl, mash the two bananas with a fork until they have completely broken down, then whisk in the eggs, followed by the milk and melted butter. Make a well in the dry ingredients, pour in the wet ones and whisk, drawing in the sides until you have a smooth batter.

Heat a teaspoon of butter in your pan (I use a cast-iron pancake pan, but a frying pan will work). Add around 50ml of the batter for each pancake and cook over a moderate flame until bubbles start to appear on the surface and the base is lightly golden. Flip over and cook the other side until lightly golden as well. Keep the pancakes warm while you cook the rest.

For each serving, place two pancakes on a plate, sandwiching a few slices of banana in the middle, scoop a tablespoon of peanut butter on top and drizzle with the syrup.

MAKES 8 LARGE-ISH PANCAKES

1 rounded tbsp unsalted butter,
   plus more to cook
200g plain flour, sifted
good pinch of salt
3 tbsp caster sugar
1½ tsp baking powder
good pinch of cumin seeds
2 large, ripe bananas
2 large eggs
300ml whole milk

TO SERVE
1 ripe banana, cut on the diagonal
   into thin slices
4 rounded tbsp unsweetened chunky
   peanut butter
natural maple syrup

I know this isn't Indian in origin, but it is so delicious I couldn't resist putting it in the book. I made this compote to go with my kulfi (see page 169), but it was even more divine eaten for breakfast the next morning. Granola is so easy to make that, once you've done it, you will never buy it again. Here it adds a lovely crunch. I like it with pistachios, almonds, cashews, pumpkin and sunflower seeds, but use your own favourite nuts and seeds. I haven't added dried fruit to it as there is some in the compote, but you can add raisins, dried cherries, dried blueberries or any other you like, with the coconut.

Blackberry-violet compote and easy granola

To make the granola, preheat the oven to 140°C/275°F/gas mark 1. Mix the oats, nuts and seeds, cinnamon and salt in a baking tray. Make a well in the middle, pour in all the wet ingredients and mix well. Bake for 40 minutes, stirring every eight to nine minutes. Add the coconut when there are five minutes to go. Take out of the oven once golden; it will crisp up as it cools. Once cold, store in an airtight container.

Place the blackberries in a saucepan with a good splash of water and heat until they start to soften. Add the syrup and dried fruit and cook for another minute, then take off the heat. Add another splash of water if the fruit looks a little dry. Taste and balance the flavours, adding more syrup or a squeeze of orange juice to balance the sweetness. Serve the compote hot or cold with Greek yogurt and the granola.

MAKES ENOUGH FOR 4

FOR THE GRANOLA
160g old-fashioned rolled oats
80g mixed nuts and seeds
½ tsp ground cinnamon
good pinch of salt
¾ tsp vanilla essence
1½ tbsp vegetable oil
55–60ml natural maple syrup
1½ tbsp honey
20g coconut flakes or desiccated coconut

FOR THE REST
400g blackberries, washed
4–5 tbsp violet syrup, or to taste
large handful of dried blueberries or raisins
squeeze of orange juice (if needed)
Greek yogurt, to serve

These are known as chillas and are a high-protein, gluten-free savoury pancake. They are eaten as they are, with spicy ketchup or chutney (see below), for breakfast or as a snack. Very quick to make, the pancakes are nutritious and filling, so are popular in vegetarian Indian homes. I also love them for an easy lunch with some simple vegetables on the side.

Spicy, crisp chickpea pancakes

Whisk 120–140ml of water into the gram flour, making sure there are no lumps. Add all the remaining ingredients except the oil and mix well. Taste for seasoning and adjust if necessary. The batter should have the consistency of double cream.

Heat around ½–¾ tsp of the oil in a cast-iron griddle pan and pour in one-quarter of the batter, to make a pancake about 15cm in diameter. Cook for one to two minutes, or until lightly golden on the base, then drizzle another ½–¾ tsp of oil over the top and flip the pancake over. Cook, pressing down to help the edges crisp up. Once the base is golden, take out and repeat with the remaining oil and batter.

Serve hot, with spicy ketchup or Coastal Coconut Chutney (see below).

MAKES 4 PANCAKES

100g gram (chickpea) flour
½ tsp cumin seeds
¼ tsp carom seeds
1½ tsp peeled and grated root ginger
2 garlic cloves, peeled and grated
salt, to taste
¼ tsp turmeric
2 tbsp chopped coriander leaves
½ onion, finely chopped
1 small tomato, chopped
2 tsp lemon juice
1–2 tbsp vegetable oil

Coastal coconut chutney
MAKES 180ML

A really lovely chutney from the South, this adds texture, creaminess and heat.

Place 100g grated coconut, 1–2 green chillies, 8g peeled root ginger, a pinch of salt, and 100g creamy Greek yogurt in a blender. Dry roast 1½ tbsp Bengal gram (chana dal) until coloured all over, then tip into the blender with 1 tbsp lemon juice. Blend until smooth, adding water to help. Heat 1 tsp vegetable oil in a saucepan, then add ⅔ tsp mustard seeds. When the popping dies down, add 8 curry leaves and cook for 10 seconds longer. Pour this into the chutney and stir it all together. Taste, adjust the seasoning and lemon juice, then serve

Kedgeree is such a British institution that I felt some trepidation in giving it my own Indian twist… the irony of this does not escape me! But I did. This is a creamy version, based on a South Indian breakfast dish. It is nutritious and filling but not heavy.

Creamy kedgeree

Place the rice and lentils in a saucepan and wash them well. Drain, add the milk and 800ml of water and bring to a boil. Reduce the heat and simmer, partially covered, until just cooked (around 10 minutes).

Meanwhile, heat 4 tbsp of the ghee or butter in a separate saucepan and add the cumin seeds. Once they darken, add the onion and cook until turning golden brown. Add the garlic and ginger and cook gently until the garlic just starts to colour. Stir in the ground spices and salt and cook for another minute. Pour in a splash of water.

By now the lentils and rice should be cooked. Stir in the spiced onions and cook for another few minutes. Add the lemon juice, herbs and cashews, taste and adjust the seasoning and consistency; it should be thick and creamy but not loose, so add a little water, or boil off extra over a high heat, as necessary. Cover as you fry your eggs.

Heat the remaining ghee or butter in a non-stick frying pan. Crack in the eggs and sizzle until the whites are cooked and the yolks still soft (I like crispy edges, too). Sprinkle over a little salt, pepper and chilli powder. Mound the rice on warm plates, top with the eggs and serve.

SERVES 4

200g basmati rice
100g yellow lentils (mung dal)
500ml whole milk
6 tbsp ghee or unsalted butter
1 tsp cumin seeds
1 large onion, chopped
4 garlic cloves, peeled and finely chopped
1 tbsp peeled and finely chopped root ginger
½ tsp turmeric
⅔ tsp freshly ground black pepper,
   plus more for the eggs
1 rounded tsp garam masala
1½ tsp ground coriander
1½ tsp ground cumin
salt, to taste
4 tsp lemon juice, or to taste
large handful of chopped chives or parsley
   (coriander is a little strong for this dish)
large handful of roasted cashews (optional)
4 large eggs
pinch of chilli powder

Masala baked beans
SERVES 4

My husband's family only eat baked beans like this. Serve on wholemeal toast for brunch.

Heat 2 tsp vegetable oil and a good knob of unsalted butter in a pan. Add 1 small red onion, finely chopped, 6g root ginger, peeled and grated, and 2 thin green chillies, deseeded and finely chopped. Sauté for two minutes. Add 2 large garlic cloves, peeled and grated, and sauté until just colouring. Tip in 2 x 400g cans of baked beans, then fill a can with water and pour this in, too. Bring to the boil and simmer for two minutes. Add 80g mature cheddar, grated, and stir until creamy.

Indians eat spiced potatoes for breakfast in their dosas (a crisp South Indian pancake), and the Parsi people love them sautéed, with eggs on top, but this recipe is inspired by American hashed potatoes. They are lovely with the omelette here but also with Masala Baked Beans (see page 20). This omelette is simply one of my favourite meals, and comes into play well beyond breakfast time. It is cooked until golden on both sides, and is spongy rather than soft. It's truly delicious.

My Indian potato hash and masala omelette

Bring the potatoes to the boil in a pan of water and boil for 15 minutes, or until just cooked through. Once cool enough to handle, grate on the coarse side of a box grater. (I grate the skin too, as I like it and it's full of fibre.) Set aside.

Heat 1 tbsp of the oil in a non-stick frying pan. Add the cumin seeds and, once they start to colour and become aromatic, add the onion. Sauté for three to four minutes, or until soft and colouring on the edges, then add the garlic. Cook for another minute or until the garlic is beginning to colour. Add everything else except the potato and sauté for 20 seconds. Stir into the potato and mix well. Taste for seasoning and adjust if necessary. Tip out on to a plate, then form the mixture into four evenly sized patties. Wipe out the pan.

Heat the remaining oil in the pan until hot, then add the potato patties and cook, undisturbed, over a medium-low flame for two or three minutes, or until golden on the bottom. Flip over and repeat. Remove them from the pan, placing on kitchen paper to absorb excess oil.

Meanwhile, mix the onion, tomatoes, chilli(es) and coriander into the eggs and beat again, then season to taste with salt.

Melt a knob of butter in a non-stick frying pan. Pour in one-quarter of the omelette mixture and cook gently, undisturbed, for one to two minutes or until the base is golden, then flip over and cook the other side until golden too. I normally slide it on to a plate and then pop it back into the pan to stop it breaking. Serve immediately with a potato hash cake, while you cook the other omelettes.

SERVES 4

FOR THE HASH
2 potatoes (around 400g in total), scrubbed well
3 tbsp vegetable oil
½ tsp cumin seeds
1 small red onion, finely chopped
2 small garlic cloves, peeled and finely chopped
½ tsp ground cumin
¼ tsp chilli powder
¼ tsp turmeric
½ tsp dried mango powder (if you have it)
⅔ tsp ground coriander
salt, to taste
2 tbsp chopped coriander leaves

FOR THE OMELETTE
1 red onion, finely chopped
2 small ripe tomatoes, chopped
1–4 green chillies, finely chopped (deseeded if you prefer), or to taste
8 tbsp finely chopped coriander leaves
8 large eggs, beaten
a few knobs of unsalted butter

These are eaten with Masala Chai (see below), as biscotti are taken with coffee in Italy. I always ate these biscuits at relatives' homes in India; they are quite addictive, not too crunchy, not too soft and not too sweet. I've rediscovered them recently and they are as moreish now as they were then. I like them plain, but you can further embellish them with nuts as if they were biscotti, if you prefer.

Indian tea biscuits

Butter a 17.5cm square tin and line with baking parchment. Preheat the oven to 180°C/350°F/gas mark 4. Beat the sugar and butter until soft and creamy. Beat in the eggs, one at a time. Sift the flour with the baking powder and add to the mixture with the salt and spice, if using. Mix well, then stir in the milk. Pour the batter into the tin, place on the middle shelf of the oven and cook for 30–35 minutes, or until a toothpick in the centre comes out clean and it is springy to touch.

Once it is cool enough to handle, halve the cake, then cut across into 2cm-thick biscuits. Place cut side down on a baking sheet. Reduce the oven temperature to 150°C/300°F/gas mark 2 and bake the biscuits for 70–80 minutes, or until they are golden with browned edges. (You can bake them for less time for a softer biscuit.)

Cool and store in an airtight tin. They last well for two weeks.

MAKES AT LEAST 20

90g unsalted butter, softened,
   plus more for the tin
95g caster sugar
3 eggs
120g plain flour
¾ tsp baking powder
pinch of salt
½ tsp ground cardamom or ginger (optional)
2 tbsp whole milk

Masala chai

I am a tea drinker and sweet-spiced Indian chai, with a hint of heat from ginger and pepper, is the ultimate revive-relax drink; it is a wondrous thing. I normally make mine with root ginger and whole spices, but this way is so much quicker and easier that it soon weaves its way into your morning.

Grind together 1½ tbsp green cardamom pods, 2 tsp fennel seeds, 1 rounded tsp ground ginger, ½ tsp black peppercorns, 6 cloves and a 6cm cinnamon stick in a spice or coffee grinder, until you have a fine powder. Store in a jar, away from sunlight.

To make tea for one, pour 250ml of water and 3 tbsp milk into a small saucepan. Add ½ tsp tea leaves and ½ tsp of the chai powder. Bring to the boil and simmer until the colour of the tea is to your liking. Pour through a small sieve into your cup. Sweeten to taste with sugar and add a little more chai powder if you like.

DRINKS

When I started developing this juice I had no idea how delicious it would be. It reminds me of the fresh sugar cane juice we would get at juice stalls in India, even though I have no idea if the stallholders added ginger to theirs. Indian juices often had a pinch of salt and pepper in them; the salt was to replenish minerals lost through sweat. It doesn't taste salty but seems to heighten the sweet, sour flavour of the fruit. It is of course optional and an acquired taste, though one I associate with my visits to India. You need a sweet, aromatic melon, such as cantaloupe, galia or honeydew.

Melon and ginger sharbat

Blend the melon, ginger, sugar and orange juice together until smooth. Add the lemon juice if the orange isn't very tart. Adjust the sugar and ginger to taste.

Add salt and pepper for a more authentic experience and pour the sharbat over ice-laden glasses.

SERVES 4

2.5kg melon flesh
30–35g root ginger, peeled weight, or to taste
4 tsp caster sugar, or to taste
juice of 2 oranges
squeeze of lemon juice (if necessary)
pinch of salt (optional)
pinch of freshly ground black pepper
    (optional)
lots of ice

Pomegranate sharbat

Try to buy organic or unwaxed citrus fruits. If these aren't available, scrub the citrus very well inded, to remove wax.
Pour as much pure pomegranate juice into a jug, or individual glasses, as you need.
Cut thin slices from a lemon, a lime and an orange. Add to the jug with a small fistful of whole mint leaves and allow the juice to sit for at least 15 minutes to infuse, before serving with ice.

Mangoes are known as the king of fruit in India and, for me, the world. There is nothing better than a mango languorously ripening in my fruit basket, while the sight of boxes of Indian mangoes in springtime cheers me up no end and reminds me of sunnier days to come. There are lots of varieties. Alphonso is my all-time favourite, but there are others that come a close second and third. When making these drinks, use a full-flavoured ripe fruit, or you will end up with something merely ordinary. The flavour of mango just needs enhancement, not masking. This is a healthy, easy breakfast for when you are in a hurry or cannot face food first thing in the morning.

Mango, honey and rose smoothie

Take the flesh off the mangoes: working above your blender, cut the cheeks from the mangoes as close to the stone as possible. Halve these lengthways. Cut or peel off the skin, making sure the juices flow into the blender. Peel off the skin around the stone and cut off as much as you can of the musky fruit from around it. Add this to the blender, too.

Add everything else and blend until smooth, adding 8–12 tbsp of water to the blender to help, if necessary. (You may need to do this in batches, to avoid overloading the blender and splattering the kitchen.) Taste, adjust the honey if you want a sweeter drink, and add more water if it is too thick, then serve.

MAKES 4 LARGE GLASSES

4 juicy, ripe mangoes
640–720g yogurt (depending how tart it is)
3 tsp rose essence or rose water
24 blanched almonds
4 tsp honey, or to taste

Saffron 'aamraas'
MAKES 4 SMALL GLASSES

'Aam' means mangoes and 'raas' means juice. There are many in India who make this as a thick purée and eat it with bread, but I have always had it thinned down as a drink. It's best in small portions with lots of ice, and is a great summer drink to serve in a large jug for guests. Saffron may seem an indulgent ingredient here, but it really complements the mango.

Prepare two mangoes as above. Bring 400ml of milk to the boil with a pinch of saffron, then reduce the heat, simmer and reduce to half its original quantity, stirring all the time. Then pour on to the mangoes in a blender and blend until smooth. Taste, add 2 tsp of caster sugar if necessary, then chill. To serve, add cold milk or water to reach a consistency you like, and serve on lots of ice.

This traditional lassi is very popular in the northern region of Punjab, where field workers would replenish themselves with both salt and sugar while cooling their bodies with mint and cumin seeds.

Sweet and savoury mint lassi

Blend together most of the yogurt with 480ml of water, the sugar, salt, cumin and half the mint. (You may need to do this in two batches, to avoid overloading the blender and splattering the kitchen.)

Stir in the remaining mint, taste and adjust the sweetness and yogurt. Chill, then serve in glasses with the ice.

SERVES 4

720g yogurt (if it is quite tart, add
   600–640g and adjust at the end)
8 tsp caster sugar, or to taste
pinch of salt
1⅓–2 tsp roasted ground cumin (see page 9)
8 tbsp shredded mint leaves or dried mint,
   crumbled in, to taste
crushed or shaved ice, to serve

A really lovely, fragrant and delicate lassi, delicious at any time of the day and with any Indian meal.

Cardamom, almond and rose lassi

Blend the yogurt, milk, almonds, cardamom, rose water and sugar together until smooth. (You may need to do this in two batches, to avoid overloading the blender and splattering the kitchen.)

Put the ice and rose petals, if using, into glasses, then pour in the lassi and serve.

SERVES 4

600g yogurt (not too sour)
500ml semi-skimmed milk
24 blanched almonds
1–1½ tsp ground cardamom
½–1½ tsp rose water, or to taste
4–5 tbsp caster sugar, or to taste
handful of crushed ice or ice cubes
organic rose petals (optional)

When visiting India as a teenager, I became obsessed with cold coffee and ice cream. South Indian coffee is delicious and once you added milk, ice cream and sugar, it was divine... I suppose it was the original iced frappuccino. I have added cinnamon and cardamom and it is quite wonderful. Like a cherry on top, I like to finish it with a sprinkling of cocoa. I don't have a coffee machine, so I use instant. If you can make fresh coffee at home, use 400ml of strong coffee instead, it will be even better.

Spiced coffee and vanilla float

Stir the coffee into 400ml of boiling water with the sugar and spices. Once well mixed, add the milk. Leave to cool, then chill.

Once cold, pour into glasses with the ice-cubes and scoop the ice cream carefully on top. Sprinkle with a little cocoa or cinnamon. Serve immediately, with a straw and a spoon.

SERVES 4

5 tsp instant coffee, or to taste (or filter coffee or espresso, see recipe introduction)
7 tsp caster sugar, or to taste
a few pinches of ground cardamom
1 tsp ground cinnamon, or to taste
 (I like a little more)
600ml semi-skimmed milk
8 ice cubes
4 small scoops of good-quality
 vanilla ice cream
cocoa powder or ground cinnamon, to serve

Iced lemon, ginger and mint tea
SERVES 3–4

A lovely, refreshing drink for a summer's day in the garden. Once cold, taste and see if you'd like more ginger. Feel free to use your favourite tea bags. Try the drink, without the tea, for children.

   Place 2 tea bags (I like Assam) in 500ml of boiling water and leave to steep for three minutes. Meanwhile, lightly bruise seven or eight ginger slices, skin on, so they release their lovely juices. Squeeze out the water from the tea bags and keep them aside (in case you want the tea stronger at the end). Add 80–90g caster sugar to the tea and stir to dissolve. Add 3 tbsp of lemon juice and pour the whole thing into a jug in which there is a good handful of ice, 500ml of cold water, the ginger and the leaves from 3–4 sprigs of mint. Stir, then chill. Before serving, add lemon slices, taste and adjust the sugar (you will need to dissolve any extra sugar in hot water first), lemon and mint to taste.

STARTERS
AND SNACKS

One of India's favourite street foods, this is a deeply satisfying combination of sweet, tangy, spicy and crunchy. It is typically tea time fare and I often make a large bowl when I have friends over, but I also love to eat a big portion for a light summer lunch. Most Indian stores sell a ready made bag of bhel mix, consisting of puffed rice, sev (small gram flour vermicelli) and papri (little rounds of crispy dough). If you cannot get this, buy the three items separately. The bhel puri is best assembled just before eating, as the puffed rice softens as it sits, but you can have the elements ready to mix together. You can also buy the chutneys from some Indian grocers if you do not feel like making your own.

Mumbai bhel puri

Have all the ingredients chopped and ready and, when you want to eat, mix the whole thing together and serve immediately, sprinkled with a little extra sev if you have it.

SERVES 4

Tangy herb chutney
MAKES 200ML

The cornerstone of all North Indian snacks. We love it with samosas, bhajis, pakoras, kebabs... and most other things.

Put 60g of coriander leaves with some of the stalks in a blender, and add 2 tbsp of lemon juice, 1 deseeded green chilli, 20g of mint leaves, 25g of pistachios, ½ garlic clove, 1 tbsp of yogurt and ½–¾ tsp of caster sugar, to taste. Add 4 tbsp of water and blend until very smooth and creamy. Taste and adjust the seasoning, adding more chilli or sugar as you prefer. Keep in the fridge, or freeze, until ready to use.

Instant tamarind chutney
MAKES 80–90ML

A really quick sweet-sour chutney, used in India almost as ketchup is in the west. It keeps well in the fridge for a month, or freezes well too.

Put 4 generous tsp of good-quality tamarind paste in a small saucepan with 150ml of water. Add 75–80g of jaggery or dark muscovado sugar, 1½ tsp of roasted cumin seeds (see page 9), and up to ½ tsp each of salt and freshly ground black pepper. Bring to the boil and simmer for five to seven minutes, or until it is a little syrupy. It will thicken further as it cools. Taste and adjust the seasoning (different brands of tamarind will vary in strength and tartness), then serve, or store in the fridge, or freeze.

225g bhel puri mix (if you can't get the mix, see recipe introduction)
large handful of roasted peanuts, skins removed by rolling between your palms
1 large-ish potato, cooked and finely chopped
1 small red onion, finely chopped
1 tomato, finely chopped
large handful of chopped coriander leaves
1–2 green chillies, deseeded and chopped
¾ tbsp lemon juice, or to taste
1½ tbsp Tangy Herb Chutney (see left)
3 tbsp Instant Tamarind Chutney (see below left)
pomegranate seeds (optional but lovely)
handful of sev, to serve (optional)

These are absolutely delicious and easy to make with simple everyday ingredients (gram flour is a must in all vegetarian households). They are soft and creamy on the inside but with a lovely crisp exterior. I use a good-quality, thick Greek yogurt and cheddar cheese instead of the traditional paneer, to add a lovely savoury element. Eat these as they are, or with Basil Chutney (see below).

Savoury yogurt kebabs

The night before, put the Greek yogurt in a sieve lined with muslin, place over a bowl and leave in the fridge overnight.

The next day, add the gram flour to a non-stick frying pan and stir over a gentle heat until it has a toasted smell and turns a golden colour, four to five minutes. Scrape into a large bowl. Clean the pan and heat 1 tbsp of the oil. Add the onion; cook gently until just softened. Add the garlic, ginger and salt and cook until the garlic no longer smells raw, 40–50 seconds. Stir in the garam masala and roasted ground cumin, take off the heat and add to the gram flour with the drained yogurt, cheese, three-quarters of the breadcrumbs, the coriander, green chilli and black pepper. Stir well and season to taste. It should be creamy but firm enough to roll into balls. If not, add more crumbs. Give the pan a good wipe.

Heat half the remaining oil in the pan until hot. Make little balls of the mixture, flatten and add a batch to the pan. Cook over a gentle flame until the bases are golden brown. Flip over and cook until this side is golden too. Drain on kitchen paper. Repeat, using more oil and kebabs, until they are all cooked. Serve with Basil Chutney (see below).

MAKES 10–12 SMALL KEBABS

220g Greek yogurt
40g gram (chickpea) flour
3 tbsp vegetable oil
½ onion, finely chopped
2 garlic cloves, peeled and finely chopped
10g root ginger, peeled weight,
    finely chopped
salt, to taste
¾ tsp garam masala, or to taste
½ tsp roasted ground cumin (see page 9)
30g mature cheddar cheese, finely grated
2 slices of white bread, crumbed,
    plus more if needed
2 tbsp chopped coriander leaves
½–1 green chilli, deseeded and finely
    chopped (optional)
freshly ground black pepper

Basil chutney
MAKES ENOUGH TO GO WITH THE KEBABS

You'll need a really large bunch of basil for this; it should weigh 70g. Pick the leaves from the basil and place in a mini food processor. Add 15 pistachios, 1 small garlic clove, peeled, and 1½ tbsp of extra virgin olive oil. Process, adding a splash of water to help the blades go round if necessary. Taste, and adjust the seasoning with lemon juice.

I first ate a momo when a Nepalese lady was helping me at home with my first baby six years ago. She did lots of chopping, then 10 minutes later had made her momos. I am dumpling-obsessed, so have dreamt of homemade momos ever since. They were brought to India by Tibetan and Nepalese people and, every time I go to Kolkata, I am tempted by the momo street vendors and restaurants catering solely to dumpling lovers. Making them is not as hard as it might seem, although your first momo will probably look quite different to your last! (See the previous page for step-by-step photos of the process.) The chutney served with this is really spicy; below is my version, but feel free to experiment.

Steamed Nepalese momos

Mix the flour with 2 tbsp of water and make a dough. Give it a good knead so it is smooth and soft, adding 1 tsp more water if needed. Halve the dough and roll each half into a long rope. Pinch off equal tiny portions, aiming to get seven or eight from each rope. Roll each into a smooth ball and cover with a damp tea towel.

Mix all the ingredients for the filling, taste and adjust the seasoning.

Place a steamer filled with water on the heat and oil the steamer basket. Taking one ball of dough at a time, use a little flour to roll out into a very thin 6–7.5cm round. Place a generous teaspoonful of filling in the centre. Take the momo in your left hand (if right handed) and use your thumb and forefinger to enclose the filling by gathering the edges of the dough and pleating them together (or you can pleat them to look like rosebuds, see previous page). Either way, make sure the filling stays well away from the edges. Place on the oiled rack, seam side up.

Once they are all done, place in the steamer, close the lid and steam for 12–14 minutes, or until the dough is no longer sticky, then serve.

MAKES 15–16 DUMPLINGS

FOR THE DUMPLINGS
50g plain flour, plus more to dust
a little vegetable oil

FOR THE FILLING
½ onion, finely chopped
90g cabbage, finely grated, excess water
    squeezed out
½ small carrot, finely grated, excess water
    squeezed out
small handful of frozen peas, defrosted
3 tbsp finely chopped red pepper
3 fine green beans, finely sliced
9g root ginger, peeled weight, finely chopped
2 garlic cloves, peeled and grated
1½ tsp soft unsalted butter
½ tsp salt, or to taste
good grinding of black pepper

Chilli, ginger and tomato chutney
MAKES ENOUGH TO GO WITH THE MOMOS

Heat 1 tbsp of vegetable oil in a small saucepan. Add 3 peeled garlic cloves, 18g of root ginger, peeled weight, and 2–3 green chillies, all roughly chopped, and sauté until the garlic begins to colour. Add 2 large tomatoes, roughly chopped, and salt, cover and cook down until the moisture has evaporated and the tomatoes are darkening. Add some boiled water and blend together (it doesn't have to be too fine). Add 1 tsp of finely chopped ginger and 1 tbsp of chopped coriander leaves. Taste, adjust the seasoning and add more finely diced green chilli, if you like. It should be loose but not watery, quite hot and gingery and slightly salty, as the dumplings are quite simple.

A much-loved snack or appetiser. I find myself returning to them even though there are newer recipes to choose from. They are crisp and delicious and best served hot in batches as soon as they are done. I have paired them with this lovely caper berry chutney. I absolutely love capers and they are particularly fabulous here. If you don't have any capers, you can add a little more lemon juice to the chutney instead.

Crisp onion bhajis with caper berry chutney

Heat 5cm of vegetable oil in a small saucepan.

Meanwhile, mix everything else together with your hands, squeezing the onions enough to allow their juices to come out and soften the gram flour. Form the mixture into small walnut-sized balls.

Check that the oil is ready by dropping in a little of the batter; it should start sizzling straight away. Add the balls to the hot oil in two batches. Reduce the heat to medium-low and cook for seven to eight minutes, turning, or until deep golden brown all over. Remove with a slotted spoon and drain on kitchen paper. Serve piping hot with the chutney, while you cook the next batch.

MAKES 12

vegetable oil, to deep-fry
2 red onions, finely sliced
4 tbsp chopped coriander leaves
salt, to taste
½-¾ tsp chilli powder
½ tsp turmeric
1 tsp garam masala
2 tsp ground coriander
2 tsp dried mango powder
2 tsp ground cumin
100g gram (chickpea) flour
2 garlic cloves, peeled and grated
15g root ginger, peeled weight, grated
⅓ tsp carom seeds

Caper berry chutney
MAKES 150ML

Blend 30g of coriander leaves and stalks with 20g of mint leaves, 1–2 green chillies, deseeded, 25g of pistachios, 2 tsp of lemon juice, 2 tbsp of water and 2 tbsp of small caper berries.

Adjust the seasoning. Stir in 1 tbsp of capers. Adjust the lemon, water and salt to taste (though you probably won't need salt) and serve, or refrigerate for up to a few days.

In these wonderful little cakes, the beetroot is absolutely delicious and surprises everyone who tries them. I often serve them with this Kashmiri-inspired radish and yogurt 'chutney'. I very rarely use a microwave but, when it comes to cooking potatoes in a hurry without them absorbing too much moisture, it's the ideal method.

Mini beetroot cakes with radish and yogurt 'chutney'

Heat half the oil in a non-stick frying pan. Add the onion and sauté for two minutes. Add the ginger and garlic and sauté until the garlic smells cooked and turns lightly golden.

Grate the beetroot, squeeze out the excess juice (I squeeze it over a cup and drink the fresh beetroot juice as I cook) and add to the pan with the garam masala, cumin, chilli powder and salt. Sauté until the moisture dries up, then add a good splash of water, cover and cook until the beetroot is just soft, adding more splashes of water as you need; it can take around 30 minutes. Cook off all the excess moisture. Add the cooked potato and mash the whole thing together; it doesn't have to be smooth. Cook off any excess moisture if the mixture seems wet.

Put the mixture on a plate and wipe the pan clean. Make little cakes out of the mix, about 3cm wide and 1cm thick. Heat the remaining oil in the pan and add the cakes. Cook over a medium flame until they are lightly crisp on the bottom but have not coloured too much. Turn over and cook for another two to three minutes. Meanwhile, stir together all the ingredients for the chutney and season to taste. Serve the beetroot cakes with a little of the chutney on top.

MAKES 12–14

FOR THE BEETROOT CAKES
3 tbsp vegetable oil
1 small red onion, chopped
2 rounded tsp peeled, grated root ginger
2 garlic cloves, peeled and grated
250g small-ish raw beetroot, peeled
½–¾ tsp garam masala, or to taste
good pinch of cumin or caraway seeds
¼ tsp chilli powder, or to taste,
    plus a little more to serve
salt, to taste
2 potatoes, cooked and peeled
    (see recipe introduction)

FOR THE RADISH AND YOGURT 'CHUTNEY'
3 large radishes, coarsely grated
90g Greek yogurt
60g crème fraîche
2 tbsp finely chopped coriander leaves
1 spring onion, green part only, finely sliced
1 green chilli, deseeded and chopped
    (optional)

Mini chilli cheese toasts
MAKES 12-14 SMALL TOASTS

I've never met anyone who doesn't like these. You can serve big slices of it for lunch, with a green salad.

Preheat the oven to its highest setting. Slice a baguette 1cm thick. Place on the upper oven shelf to toast. Mix ¾ small red onion, finely chopped, 1 small tomato, finely chopped, ¼–½ green chilli, finely chopped, 2 tbsp of chopped coriander leaves, a pinch of salt and 120g of grated cheddar. Mound on to the toasts and cook until the cheese melts and there are a few speckled brown bits on top. Bits of the cheese will spill on to the baking tray. They're my favourite!

Fluffy, spongy, savoury cakes from the region of Gujarat. These are made with yellow lentils (mung dal), which are really light and mild in flavour, so perfect once steeped in this spicy rasam broth. You need a 20cm round cake tin with a fixed base and a large, deep saucepan or wok with a lid, into which such a cake tin will fit. Then you need to find something on which to place the tin so that it does not touch the water. Any heatproof bowl (I use pudding bowls) or colander will work.

Steamed lentil cakes in sweet, spicy, sour rasam

Drain the soaked lentils and put them in a blender (or put them in a bowl and use a stick blender). Add the ginger, chillies, salt, sugar, oil, lemon juice and 100–110ml of water and blend to a paste. Mix in the bicarbonate of soda and leave for 15 minutes.

Meanwhile, find a wide, large double boiler or deep and large saucepan, big enough to take your cake tin. Find something to place the tin on, so its base is above the level of the water (pudding bowls, steel baking rings and upturned colanders are all good). Pour in enough water to come 5cm up the pan. Cover the pan tightly and bring to the boil.

Pour the batter into an oiled 20cm cake tin, place it carefully on its stand in the pan, cover and steam until an inserted toothpick comes out clean, 10–12 minutes. Take off the lid, allow the steam to escape and carefully take out the pan (I use oven gloves and tongs).

For the rasam, heat the oil in a small non-stick saucepan. Add the mustard seeds and, once the popping is dying down, add the curry leaves. Follow a few seconds later with the tomato, spices and salt. Cook over a high to moderate heat for three to four minutes, stirring often, then add 360ml of water. Bring to the boil, reduce the heat and simmer for 10 minutes. Stir in the sugar and tamarind and simmer for another minute; it should be a little sweet, sour and spicy. Adjust the salt, sugar, chilli powder and tamarind as you like. Turn off the heat.

Cut the lentil cake into 5cm squares or half moons, place in deep warmed bowls and spoon over a little of the rasam. Leave to soak for four to five minutes, then sprinkle with coriander and coconut, if you have some, and serve.

SERVES 4

FOR THE LENTIL CAKES

200g yellow lentils (mung dal), washed well
    and soaked overnight
10g root ginger, peeled weight
2 thin green chillies, stalks removed
    and deseeded
1 rounded tsp salt, or to taste
3 tsp caster sugar
1 tbsp vegetable oil, plus more for the tin
1 tbsp lemon juice
⅔ tsp bicarbonate of soda

FOR THE RASAM

1 tbsp vegetable oil
¾ tsp mustard seeds
8 fresh curry leaves (or 12 dried)
1 large tomato, chopped
2 tsp ground coriander
1 tsp ground cumin
½–¾ tsp chilli powder, or to taste
salt, to taste
1–1½ tbsp caster sugar, to taste
1½–1¾ tsp tamarind paste dissolved in
    3 tbsp boiling water, or to taste
coriander leaves, to serve (optional)
fresh, or frozen and defrosted, grated
    coconut, to serve (optional)

A restaurant vegetarian favourite, these are normally tunnelled out and stuffed with a mixture of paneer, cashew nuts, raisins and the fried potato scraps. This was the initial inspiration for this dish, but these are much easier, lighter and tastier. They make great, easy appetisers or a wonderful side dish, if made with larger potatoes, for a barbecue.

Tandoori baby potatoes with herb yogurt

Peel the potatoes and halve. Bring lots of salted water to the boil in a large saucepan. Add the potatoes and boil for eight minutes. Remove and, when cool enough to handle, use a spoon to scrape out a deep depression so that the potatoes look like boiled egg halves where the yolk has been removed.

Mix the ingredients for the tandoori marinade in a bowl. Add one good tsp of salt (the marinade only coats the potato so the salt will not seem excessive). Place the potato halves in the bowl, turn to coat in the marinade and leave to marinate for 30 minutes. Mix together all the ingredients for the topping, adding the milk if the consistency seems a little thick, and season to taste.

Preheat the oven to 220°C/425°F/gas mark 7. Place the potatoes, flat side up, on a baking tray and place on the middle shelf of the oven. Cook for 20–25 minutes, or until the marinade looks properly dried. Now turn the potatoes over, move the rack to the top of the oven, and continue to cook for eight to 10 minutes. Turn again and cook for a final eight to 10 minutes. They should be tender by now (check by piercing one of the largest potato halves with a knife).

Meanwhile, melt the butter and brush it over the potatoes. Spoon a rounded tsp of topping on to each potato half and serve immediately.

MAKES 16 HALVES

FOR THE POTATOES
8 baby potatoes
salt
2 tbsp unsalted butter

FOR THE TANDOORI MARINADE
150g Greek yogurt
1¾ tsp ground cumin
¾ tsp garam masala
1 tsp ground coriander
¼–½ tsp chilli powder
1 tsp paprika
3 garlic cloves, peeled and grated
7g root ginger, peeled weight, grated
2 tbsp vegetable oil
1½ tbsp lemon juice, or to taste

FOR THE TOPPING
250g Greek yogurt
⅓ tsp freshly ground black pepper
good handful of chopped coriander leaves
½–¾ small onion, finely chopped
1 green chilli, deseeded and finely chopped, or to taste
2 tbsp dried cranberries or raisins (optional, for a sweet/savoury combination)
1–2 tbsp whole milk, if needed

I loved Scotch eggs when I visited England in my summer holidays as a teenager. I wanted them for a snack, on picnics and as part of my lunch! They were so very British to me. So British, in fact, that they were brought to Kolkata during the Raj and can now be seen on some menus in that corner of India. I use quail's eggs, but you can use hen's eggs instead and serve them with a salad for lunch or brunch. If you do not eat eggs, make this vegetarian sausagemeat into kebabs instead: add a diced tomato to the mixture, shape on to skewers and cook in the oven or in a frying pan.

Scotch quail's eggs

Heat 2 tsp of the oil in a small non-stick frying pan and fry the garlic until colouring. Then tip into a blender with the ginger and drained lentils and blend until smooth. Do not add any water.

Heat the remaining oil in the pan. Add the lentil paste and cook over a medium-low flame for six to seven minutes, turning often. The mixture gets tough, but you need to persevere. I spread it out in the pan, let it cook for 10 seconds, turn it, then repeat. Keep moving and squashing it with a spoon so it cooks evenly. There is no elegant technique!

Take off the heat, add the remaining ingredients except the eggs and mix well together; it will resemble a dough. Leave to cool. At this point, you can cover the mixture and chill overnight, if it's more convenient. When you're ready to make the Scotch eggs, boil the quail's eggs for four minutes, then plunge into cold water to stop the cooking.

Peel the eggs. Take around 25–30g of the lentil mixture and flatten it in your palm. Place an egg in the middle and envelop it with the mixture. (It is easier than it sounds.) Repeat with the rest.

Meanwhile, heat 3cm of vegetable oil in a small saucepan and heat to about 180°C/350°F or until, when a scrap of bread is dropped in, it sizzles immediately but does not brown. Add the eggs, in batches, and cook over a moderate flame until they are golden all over.

Remove with a slotted spoon and drain on kitchen paper. Keep warm while you fry the remaining eggs, and serve hot as they are, or with a little Southern Tomato Chutney (see page 128).

MAKES 12

4 tbsp vegetable oil, plus more to deep-fry
4 garlic cloves, peeled and roughly sliced
20g root ginger, peeled weight
200g red lentils (masoor dal), washed well
    and soaked overnight
2 large slices of bread, crumbed
1½ tsp garam masala
1 tsp salt
large pinch of freshly ground black pepper
1½ tsp ground cumin
1 tsp chilli powder
2 tsp lemon juice
2 tbsp Greek yogurt
2 large shallots, finely chopped
    (or ½ onion)
4 tbsp finely chopped coriander leaves
12 quail's eggs

I have always loved artichokes, but had never cooked an Indian dish with them until I invented this recipe recently. The gram flour batter adds a layer of flavour which is sympathetic to the artichokes. It is daunting to prepare an artichoke if you haven't done it before, but you get used to it quickly (see below). I am quite happy to munch on these with a squeeze of lemon juice alone, but they also work with Tangy Herb Chutney (see page 34), or even a lovely garlicky mayonnaise.

Indian-style artichoke fritti

Whisk together the ingredients for the batter with 160–180ml of water until smooth. Taste and adjust the salt and chilli powder.

Heat 5cm of oil in a wide, medium-sized saucepan. Dip the artichoke slices into the batter and, using tongs, place gently in the hot oil, one at a time. Do not overcrowd the pan. Cook on a moderate flame, turning once, until the batter is deep golden on both sides, it should take three to four minutes. Drain and place on a double layer of kitchen paper. Repeat with the remaining artichoke slices. Serve immediately, with lemon wedges.

SERVES 4

FOR THE BATTER
60g gram (chickpea) flour
salt, to taste
1 tsp peeled, grated root ginger
1 tsp grated garlic
½ tsp chilli powder, or to taste
1 tsp garam masala
2 slightly rounded tsp ground coriander
2 slightly rounded tsp ground cumin
½ tsp turmeric
2 tsp dried mango powder

FOR THE REST
vegetable oil, to deep-fry
2 large globe artichokes, prepared as below
    and sliced ½cm thick
lemon wedges, to serve

How to prepare an artichoke

Fill a bowl with water and add the juice of ½ lemon. Working on one artichoke at a time, remove all the dark green leaves. (I slice through the tops then pluck out the tough green leaves until I'm left with thin, paler leaves.) Pluck these off as well, or slice through their bases with a knife. Now remove the furry choke from the centre; I find this comes out with a good scraping with a spoon, taking out all the (deceptively) soft fibres. The cut surface will start to oxidise and brown immediately, so rub it with the other lemon half to prevent discoloration. Slice off and discard most of the stem, leaving 2–3cm; peel off its tough green skin. Place straight in the lemony water until ready to use.

SALADS
AND GRILLS

This is a really fresh, vibrant and fruity salad with the grown-up edge of ginger and chilli. A good, ripe mango is important as it will add vibrancy and set off the crumbly, creamy paneer. I make my own paneer as it's **easy** and much creamier than shop bought (see page 9 for how to make it), but I leave it up to you. You can substitute mozzarella (don't grill it, of course). Lastly, find good-quality sun-dried tomatoes. I buy mine from a deli; they are more sun-blushed than dried and are moist and fresh.

Grilled paneer and mango salad with ginger dressing

Put the grill on. Whisk together the ingredients for the dressing. Make sure the sugar and salt have dissolved and the whole thing emulsifies.

If your paneer is not fresh, soak in boiling water until it softens, around 10 minutes. Then toss it in a little olive oil and season with salt and pepper. Place on an oiled rack and grill until it has browned on the edges, around seven to 10 minutes. (You can also griddle the paneer in a hot griddle pan.)

Meanwhile, toss the remaining salad ingredients with the dressing, either all together or separately, depending on how you want to present the salad. When the paneer is done, place on top. Serve immediately.

SERVES 4

FOR THE GINGER DRESSING
6–8 tsp lemon juice, to taste
6 tbsp olive oil, plus more for the paneer
salt, to taste
2 tsp caster sugar, or to taste
20g root ginger, peeled weight, finely grated

FOR THE SALAD
300g paneer (preferably homemade,
    see page 9), cut into long flat rectangles
    or other shapes
freshly ground black pepper
4 large handfuls of baby spinach or
    mixed salad leaves
110–120g sun-dried tomatoes in oil
2 large or 4 small ripe mangoes, cheeks cut
    off and diced into 1.5cm pieces
½ small red onion, finely sliced
1 mild red chilli, finely sliced (optional)
handful of chopped coriander leaves
handful of roasted peanuts or cashew nuts

This lovely, light dish started out as a simple courgette carpaccio on a summer evening when I had friends coming over. It has since morphed into a more substantial dish that works equally well as a light salad or as a platter to be eaten with grilled foods. Griddling courgette slices adds a lot of flavour. The Indian-inspired chickpea salsa is based upon a roadside chaat, but is fresher.

Griddled courgette carpaccio, chickpea salsa, pistachio dressing

Heat a griddle pan until quite hot. Slice the courgettes on the diagonal into thin slices, no more than ½cm thick. Oil the slices, place on the griddle in a single layer and cook, undisturbed, for three minutes, or until the base has well-charred lines. Turn and repeat on the other side. Repeat with the remaining courgettes. Transfer to a plate as you cook each batch.

As you stand over the griddle, stir together the chickpeas, lemon juice, roasted cumin, tomato and red onion and season to taste.

Blend together all the ingredients for the dressing with 2 tbsp water until smooth; I use a good stick blender, but a mortar and pestle will also work. Adjust the seasoning and vinegar to taste and set aside.

To assemble, place the courgettes on plates or a platter, slightly overlapping at the edges. Drizzle with the dressing. Mix the coriander into the chickpeas, scatter them over with the feta cheese and serve.

SERVES 4 AS A SIDE DISH, OR 2 AS A LIGHT LUNCH

FOR THE SALAD

4 large courgettes (a mix of green and yellow,
    if possible)
olive oil, to brush
400g can chickpeas, drained well and rinsed
1½ tbsp lemon juice, or to taste
1 scant tbsp roasted ground cumin
    (see page 9)
1 small tomato, finely chopped
⅓–½ small red onion, finely chopped
salt, to taste
30g coriander (leaves and roots), chopped
75–100g feta cheese, crumbled

FOR THE PISTACHIO DRESSING

¾–1 tbsp red or white wine vinegar,
    or to taste
1 small garlic clove, peeled
15g pistachios (roasted is fine)
2½ tbsp extra virgin olive oil
¼ tsp coarsely ground black pepper,
    or to taste
¼ tsp caster sugar

This lovely dish is a fusion of a creamy American potato salad and the potato salad from India known as aloo chaat. Chaat masala is a blend of tangy spices and literally means 'to lick' (as in your fingers). It can be found in all Indian grocers, as well as online. You can leave it out if you don't have it, the salad is still sublime and immensely moreish without overpowering the potatoes. Any waxy potatoes will work in this salad, so find out what is in season and use those as they will have the best flavour. The radishes add bite and crunch and their leaves have a lovely peppery flavour, but you can add any other vegetable you like; try finely sliced fennel, cucumbers, celery or even fine beans.

Three-seed potato salad

Place the potatoes in a large pot and cover with plenty of water, salt well and bring to the boil. Boil until the tip of a knife goes through them easily, around 15 minutes.

Meanwhile, make the dressing. Whisk together the lemon juice, mayonnaise, sour cream, garlic and half the oil, then season to taste. Heat the remaining oil in a small saucepan, tilting it so the oil collects in one area. When hot, add the mustard and cumin seeds, following after a few seconds with the fennel seeds. Reduce the heat and cook for 10 seconds or until the popping dies down. Stir into the dressing.

Drain the cooked potatoes and peel as soon as they are cool enough to handle; halve if small, or quarter larger ones. Stir into the dressing with the red onion, chillies and chaat masala, if using. The potatoes will absorb the dressing as they cool. Stir in the radishes and their leaves and the coriander just before serving. Taste and adjust the seasoning. Sprinkle with a little more chaat masala, if you like, then serve.

SERVES 4 AS A SIDE DISH

Heirloom tomato and cannellini salad
SERVES 4

Heirloom tomatoes are a motley crew. Happily, they taste great too. Serve this with griddled rustic bread.

Blend 6 tbsp of extra virgin olive oil, 3 tbsp of red wine vinegar, 1 garlic clove and 1–2 deseeded red chillies until smooth, then add salt and ¾ tsp of caster sugar. Cut 600g heirloom or baby tomatoes into wedges. Stir in ½ sliced red onion with 5 tbsp of dressing. Mix in 250g of cooked cannellini beans. Toss four handfuls of mixed leaves in a little seasoning and oil. Divide the tomato and beans between four plates. Mound the leaves on top. Break 150g of goat's curd or soft, mild goat's cheese in chunks and place on top. Grind on black pepper, drizzle with more dressing and serve.

FOR THE SALAD
500g new potatoes, washed well
salt, to taste
¼ small red onion, very finely sliced
1–2 green chillies, deseeded and finely chopped (optional)
½–¾ tsp chaat masala, plus more to serve (optional, see recipe introduction)
3 large radishes with leaves (if possible), well washed and finely sliced
large handful of chopped coriander leaves

FOR THE DRESSING
2 tsp lemon juice
4 tbsp mayonnaise (light is fine)
2 rounded tbsp sour cream
1 small-ish garlic clove, peeled and grated
1½ tbsp extra virgin olive oil
lots of freshly ground black pepper
½ tsp mustard seeds
½ tsp cumin seeds
½ tsp fennel seeds

This dried fig chutney is the perfect partner to salty, slightly squeaky Middle Eastern halloumi, though it would be wonderful with most other cheeses as well. I serve this as a light meal with herbed naan on the side, or as part of my Tandoori Vegetable Feast (see page 73). The cheese is also great with Warm Puy Lentils (see page 152) on a bed of lettuce. Panch phoran is a mixture of seeds; if you don't have it, use equal quantities of cumin, nigella, mustard and fennel seeds.

Spice-crusted halloumi with fig and pistachio chutney

For the chutney, heat the oil in a small non-stick saucepan. Add the fennel seeds and chilli powder, cook for 20 seconds, then add the onion and sauté for two or three minutes. Add the ginger and garlic and cook for another minute or until the garlic is colouring a little. Add the figs, vinegar, sugar and remaining spices along with a splash of water. Bring to a boil, then cover and cook until the figs are soft and the whole thing has come together. Taste and adjust the seasoning, seeing if you would like more sugar, vinegar or chilli powder. Blend half the chutney together until smooth, then return it to the pan and mix it with the chunky chutney. Stir in the pistachios and set aside.

Cut the halloumi into long 1cm-thick slices. Sprinkle a little of the panch phoran on one side. Heat a pan and add the oil. Add the halloumi spice side down and cook until golden on the edges, around one or two minutes. Flip over and cook this side in the same way.

Whisk together the extra virgin oil and lemon juice and season with salt and pepper. Toss the salad leaves gently in this dressing and serve with the cheese and some fig chutney on the side.

SERVES 4

FOR THE CHUTNEY
1 tbsp vegetable oil
½ tsp fennel seeds
¼ tsp chilli powder, or to taste
½ small onion, chopped
8g root ginger, peeled weight, finely chopped
2 garlic cloves, peeled and grated
100g dried figs, finely chopped
3½ tbsp red wine vinegar, or to taste
2 tsp caster sugar, or to taste
⅓ tsp garam masala
⅓ tsp roasted ground cumin (see page 9)
small fistful of pistachios

FOR THE HALLOUMI
250g packet of halloumi
1 tbsp panch phoran (see recipe introduction)
2 tsp vegetable oil
2 tbsp extra virgin olive oil
¾ tbsp lemon juice
salt, to taste
freshly ground black pepper
4 handfuls of salad leaves

Kathi rolls are one of India's indigenous 'sandwiches', in which a filling is encased in bread and designed to be eaten on the go. I was first introduced to the concept in Mumbai, when local friends would stop to buy one from a street vendor who came to the car window. They were always hot, fresh and absolutely delicious. I haven't had one for years and don't know if the 'Frankie seller' still operates, but the memory lives on. I have used a tortilla wrap here, instead of flatbread. You can use any vegetable that is not too watery and retains its texture and flavour.

Mushroom and vegetable kathi rolls

Heat 2½ tbsp of the oil in a large non-stick frying pan. Add the ginger and garlic and cook for one minute, or until the garlic is turning golden.

Add the mushrooms, vegetables and spices and a little salt. Stir-fry for five to seven minutes, or until the vegetables are cooked but still crispy. Place in a bowl and cover to keep warm. Wipe the pan clean.

Heat 1 tsp more vegetable oil in the pan, brush or spoon a good coating of egg on one side of a tortilla and place in the oil, egg side down; cook for 30 seconds or until the egg is cooked. Turn the tortilla over and cook for 30 seconds or so. Repeat with the other tortillas.

Spoon one-quarter of the filling on to each tortilla, egg side up, and cover evenly with a good tablespoon of chutney. Wrap well, halve and serve, or wrap in greaseproof paper, tearing down as you eat on the go.

MAKES 4

4 tbsp vegetable oil
16g root ginger, peeled weight, grated
4 garlic cloves, peeled and grated
16 chestnut mushrooms, cleaned and thickly sliced
1 small-ish red onion, sliced
80g carrot, cut into 5cm-long thin matchsticks
12 fine green beans, cut into 5cm-long pieces
160g white cabbage, shredded
½ red pepper, deseeded and sliced lengthways into fine matchsticks
1½ tsp chaat masala (see page 58), or to taste
1 tsp ground cumin
1 tsp ground coriander
⅔ tsp turmeric
salt, to taste
4 flour tortillas
2 small eggs, beaten with a pinch of salt
4 rounded tbsp Tangy Herb Chutney (see page 34)

Roasting or grilling mushrooms really intensifies their flavours as the heat drives out the moisture. These, in particular, are really delicious; meaty, spicy and even better if you can barbecue them, as it will add smokiness. They make a lovely starter or light meal, but they can be served without the breadcrumbs, rocket or sauce as part of a Tandoori Vegetable Feast (see page 73).

Roasted spiced portabella with creamy lemon dressing

For the crumbs, heat the butter and oil in a large frying pan. Add the garlic and fry gently until it starts to colour. Add the crumbs and stir-fry over a moderate flame until they turn golden. Take off the heat and stir in the herbs. Season to taste.

Whisk together all the ingredients for the dressing and season to taste. Blend together the ingredients for the marinade until smooth and season well. Clean the mushrooms: I like to wash them properly, as there is nothing worse than biting into gritty mushrooms. Poke through the mushrooms in several places with a small sharp blade or skewer and place them in a shallow bowl with the marinade, turning to coat on all sides. Set aside and marinate for at least 30 minutes, though an hour is better if you have the time.

Preheat the oven to 200°C/400°F/gas mark 6. Put the marinated mushrooms, gill side up, on a baking tray and roast on the upper shelf, turning halfway, for 12–15 minutes. They should look a little shrivelled at the edges.

Take out, sprinkle the gill side liberally with the crumbs, place a small fistful of rocket on the side and drizzle both with the dressing.

MAKES 4

Creamy dipping sauce
MAKES AROUND 200ML

Great with tandoori food, naan and even baked potatoes.
  Put 150g of light cream cheese in a bowl and mix together with 2–3 tbsp of milk. Season well, adding a good handful of chopped coriander leaves, ½ small onion, finely chopped, 1 green chilli, deseeded and finely chopped, and 1 tsp of lemon juice. Taste, adjust the seasoning and serve.

FOR THE GARLIC HERB CRUMBS
1 tbsp unsalted butter
1 tsp olive oil
1 fat garlic clove, peeled and grated
3 slices of bread, crumbed (not too fine)
1 rounded tbsp chopped coriander leaves
1 tbsp chopped mint leaves
salt, to taste
freshly ground black pepper

FOR THE DRESSING
1½ tsp lemon juice
1 scant tbsp crème fraîche or sour cream
3 large mint leaves, shredded
2 tbsp extra virgin olive oil

FOR THE MARINADE
2 large-ish garlic cloves, peeled
8g root ginger, peeled weight
⅓ tsp chilli powder
¾ tsp garam masala
¾ tsp ground cumin
2 tbsp lemon juice
4–5 tbsp olive oil

FOR THE MUSHROOMS
4 large-ish portabella mushrooms
  (brown-skinned are better)
2 large handfuls of baby rocket leaves

These burgers are spicy and deeply satisfying. Put aside any preconceptions of bland, mass-produced bean burgers, these are so much more. The coleslaw really adds vivacity with its texture, freshness and tanginess. The patties also work well made into kebabs and rolled into a wrap with the coleslaw, Tangy Herb Chutney (see page 34) and garlic yogurt.

Mile-high chickpea burgers with Indian purple coleslaw

For the burgers, heat 2 tbsp of the oil in a non-stick saucepan. Add the cumin seeds and cook for 10–20 seconds, or until they have darkened a little. Add the onion and cook until golden and the edges are beginning to brown. Add the ginger and garlic and cook gently for a minute or until the garlic no longer smells raw. Add the spices, salt and a splash of water and cook down until dry again.

Add the chickpeas and cook for three to four minutes, or until most of the moisture in the pan has dried off. Taste and adjust the seasoning. Pour just over three-quarters of the contents of the pan into a blender with the breadcrumbs, and blend until smooth. Lightly crush the remaining chickpeas in the saucepan, scrape the blended mixture back into the pan and mix well.

Mix together all the ingredients for the coleslaw and season to taste.

When you are ready to eat, heat the remaining oil in a non-stick frying pan. Make four to six burgers out of the chickpea mixture, making sure the edges are smooth. Place in the pan and cook over a gentle flame for six to eight minutes, turning once, until both sides are lightly browned.

Meanwhile, lightly toast your buns. Assemble the burgers as you prefer, with the coleslaw, lettuce and tomato. Balance the remaining bun half on it all and enjoy.

MAKES 4 LARGE BURGERS, OR 6 MEDIUM BURGERS

FOR THE BURGERS
4 tbsp vegetable oil
1½ tsp cumin seeds
1 small-ish onion, finely chopped
2 rounded tsp peeled, finely chopped root ginger
4 garlic cloves, peeled and finely chopped
2 tsp ground coriander
1½ tsp ground cumin
1½ tsp garam masala
1½ tsp dried pomegranate powder (optional but really delicious)
1½ tsp chilli powder
salt, to taste
2 x 400g cans chickpeas, drained and rinsed
2 slices of wholemeal bread, crumbed

FOR THE PURPLE COLESLAW
50g shredded red cabbage
20g finely sliced red onion
30g finely sliced carrots
large handful of chopped coriander leaves
80g mayonnaise (light is fine)
30g Greek yogurt
2 tsp lemon juice
freshly ground black pepper

TO SERVE
4 large, or 6 small, burger buns (I like those with sesame seeds on top)
a few crispy lettuce leaves
1 large vine tomato, sliced

This is a really popular Delhi street food and, once sweetcorn season arrives, you will find mounds of cobs on makeshift carts along the roadside, all being grilled over charcoal until the kernels are charred and lightly blistered to smoky sweetness. They are then doused in a spice blend which is rubbed in with lime wedges. We often ate this at home as a healthy snack with chaat masala, a store-bought spice blend that is spicy and sour. I don't have a garden these days so instead of barbecuing my sweetcorn, I par-boil it, then grill it over an open flame on my gas hob, turning with tongs until it has the right level of char. You can also use a griddle pan; it should take around 20 minutes.

Delhi-style grilled sweetcorn

If you are griddling the corn cobs, or cooking them over a barbecue, do so over a medium-low heat, turning often, until the kernels become golden and blister in areas.

Otherwise, place the corn cobs in a pot of boiling water, return to the boil and cook for eight to 10 minutes. Lift out, place on kitchen paper and pat dry. Now place the cobs directly on the flame of a gas hob. Turn with tongs until at least two-thirds of the corn is slightly charred.

However you chose to cook it, now rub one of the lime halves up and down each cob and sprinkle liberally all around with the chaat masala and a little chilli powder, if you like the heat. Take the used lime wedge and use it to rub this masala in really well, then serve.

MAKES 4

4 sweetcorn cobs, husks and silk removed
2 limes or lemons, halved
4 tsp chaat masala, or to taste
chilli powder, to taste

My Indian vegetarian BLT! The paneer is grilled in a spicy marinade and lightly charred; the black cardamom adds a smoky dimension. The tangy mayonnaise mixture contains some Greek yogurt for freshness and tang. All in all, this is a warm, spicy, crunchy sandwich that is very moreish. Of course, it will be better if you make your own paneer (see page 9) but, if you use shop-bought paneer, steep it in boiling water for 15 minutes to soften before marinating and cooking.

'PLT'

Stir together the yogurt, ginger, garlic, ground spices, lemon juice and oil and season to taste. Grate in the cardamom (I use a fine Microplane, but a nutmeg grater will work).

Place the paneer in the marinade and leave for at least 20 minutes. Put a piece of foil on a grill tray and turn the grill to high. Arrange the paneer slices on the rack and grill for 10 minutes, turning once, or until the edges are charring.

Meanwhile, toast the bread. Stir together the mayo, yogurt, lemon juice and milk and season lightly.

Spread the mayo over one piece of toast, place over an even layer of tomato slices, then lettuce. Top with the paneer, add the onion slices, then the last toast. Serve immediately.

MAKES 4

FOR THE MARINADE
140g Greek yogurt
1⅓ tsp peeled, grated root ginger
1 tsp grated garlic
1⅓ tsp chilli powder
1⅓ tsp ground cumin
1⅓ tsp garam masala
1⅓ tsp paprika
8 tsp lemon juice
4 tbsp vegetable oil
salt, to taste
4 black cardamom pods (optional)

FOR THE SANDWICH
300g paneer (preferably homemade,
    see page 9), cut into long 1cm slices
8 slices of wholemeal or other bread, thin or
    medium sliced
8 tsp mayonnaise (can be light)
2 tbsp Greek yogurt
4 tsp lemon juice
4 tsp whole milk, plus more if needed
2 small vine tomatoes, finely sliced
a few crisp lettuce leaves
a few finely sliced rounds of red onions,
    separated into rings

A lovely light meal which, despite having a few components, is easy to make and utterly delicious. I often serve this with Warm Puy Lentils (see page 152) or Roasted Spiced Portabella (see page 63). I have used butternut squash here as it's so widely available, but try to find different varieites, such as kabocha or acorn squash, as the contrast of green skin and orange flesh is great.

Spice-roasted butternut squash with tomatoes and capered yogurt

Preheat the oven to 190°C/375°F/gas mark 5.

Cut the squash into wedges, around 2.5–3.5cm thick. I leave the skin on. Grind the cinnamon, cloves, fennel seeds and star anise to a powder. Stir into the oil with the salt and chilli powder. Toss the squash wedges in the spiced oil, place on a roasting tray and roast for 25 minutes, or until tender to the point of a knife.

While these cook, make the yogurt. Heat the oil for the yogurt, add the capers and allow them to fry and their moisture to evaporate for two or three minutes. Stir into the yogurt with the sugar, season to taste and set aside. Wipe the pan.

Heat the oil for the tomatoes, add the panch phoran, reduce the heat and cook until the seeds stop popping. Add the tomatoes and season well. Cook for two to three minutes over a high heat, or just until the tomatoes start to soften.

Serve the squash with the tomatoes and a helping of yogurt.

SERVES 3–4, CAN BE DOUBLED

FOR THE SQUASH
500g butternut squash (weight without seeds)
7.5cm cinnamon stick
6 cloves
²⁄₃ tsp fennel seeds
1 small star anise
1½ tbsp olive oil
salt, to taste
½–¾ tsp chilli powder, or to taste

FOR THE CAPERED YOGURT
1 tbsp olive oil
1½ tbsp capers, rinsed
225g Greek yogurt
1½–1¾ tsp caster sugar, or to taste

FOR THE TOMATOES
1 tbsp olive oil
1 rounded tsp panch phoran, or use equal quantities of cumin, fennel, mustard and nigella seeds
300g baby tomatoes, halved

The sun did not have to come out in the summer for the barbecue to be lit in our home. If it was forecast to be a warm and rain-free weekend, my parents would start inviting people. I think barbecues are the best way of entertaining in summer if you have a garden, and are great for getting flavour into vegetables. Here is a lovely, easy marinade to get you started. You can grill any vegetable, this is just a list of those I enjoy with the spicy marinade. Serve with chutneys and lots of salads, such as the Ultimate Kachumber in this photo (see page 155). Definitely put some naans on to grill at the same time (see page 136), as barbecues do wonders for them.

Tandoori vegetable feast

To blanch the vegetables, bring a large pot of salted water to the boil. Throw in each vegetable, separately. Return to the boil, then time the cooking: artichokes and mushrooms take two minutes, cauliflower and asparagus take one. Remove with a slotted spoon and plunge into cold water to stop the cooking. Squeeze mushrooms to remove any excess water. Broccoli, radicchio, fennel and peppers will not need blanching.

For the marinade, place half the yogurt, the oil, lemon juice, spices, garlic, ginger and cashew nuts in a blender and blend until smooth. Stir in the remaining yogurt and season generously.

Preheat the gril to its highest setting, or light the barbecue. Oil a grill rack or a large baking tray.

Dip the vegetables in the marinade and coat well. Place on the rack or tray and barbecue or grill until the paste turns golden and charred in places. Turn and repeat; it takes around 10 minutes in total.

Baste the vegetables with butter and serve with the lemon wedges and Creamy Mint Chutney (see below).

SERVES 4

FOR THE VEGETABLES
salt
700g vegetables, such as:
   artichoke hearts
   mushrooms
   cauliflower, in large florets
   asparagus spears
   broccoli, in large florets
   purple radicchio or endive, cut into wedges
      through the root
   fennel, cut into 1cm slices
   peppers, quartered lengthways
a little vegetable oil
2–3 tbsp melted unsalted butter, to baste
lemon wedges, to serve

FOR THE TANDOORI MARINADE
300g plain yogurt
3 tbsp vegetable oil
3 tbsp lemon juice
3 tsp ground cumin
½–¾ tsp chilli powder, or to taste
1 tsp garam masala, or to taste
$^2/_3$ tsp ground cardamom
4 garlic cloves, peeled and grated
15g root ginger, peeled weight, grated
50g cashew nuts, soaked for 10 minutes,
   then drained
good pinch of freshly ground black pepper

Creamy mint chutney
MAKES AROUND 250ML

This is the type of chutney, called pudina, that you find in Indian restaurants to eat with your popadums. It's great with tandoori food.
   Blend together 30g of mint leaves, 30g of coriander leaves and stalks, 2 tsp of roasted ground cumin (see page 9), 1 tbsp of caster sugar, 1 green chilli, deseeded, and 50g of yogurt until smooth. Season with salt, then stir in 150g more yogurt and lemon juice to taste. Adjust the seasoning and serve.

GLORIOUS VEGETABLES

I absolutely love this. It's a very Punjabi dish known as bharta in India, and it's great with lentil and bean curries, or just with crispy naan or flatbreads and some creamy raita.

Smoky spiced aubergines

Smear the aubergines with a little oil, place directly over a gas flame and cook, turning often, until charred all over. It will take around 15 minutes. (Or roast them in the oven at 220°C/425°F/gas mark 7 for 25–30 minutes.) Sprinkle water all over and leave to cool.

Meanwhile, heat the ghee in a non-stick saucepan. Add the onions and chillies and cook until soft. Add the ginger and garlic and cook, stirring, for a minute or so. Add the tomatoes, spices and salt and cook until the tomatoes release oil back into the pan, stirring occasionally. This should take about 15 minutes.

Meanwhile, peel the skin from the aubergines and discard. Chop the flesh and add it to the tomato saucepan with any juices that have accumulated in the aubergine dish, then tip in the peas. Cook over a medium-low heat, stirring occasionally, for 15–20 minutes, until the moisture has dried off and the mixture looks creamy. Cover and leave to rest for five minutes, then stir in the chopped coriander and serve.

SERVES 4 GENEROUSLY

2 large aubergines
a little vegetable oil
3 tbsp ghee (or half oil, half butter)
2 small-ish onions, finely chopped
1–3 green chillies, whole but pierced with the tip of a knife
20g root ginger, peeled weight, finely chopped
2 garlic cloves, peeled and finely chopped
4 tomatoes, chopped
2 rounded tsp ground coriander
1 tsp ground cumin
¾ tsp garam masala
salt, to taste
2 large handfuls of green peas (I use frozen)
handful of chopped coriander leaves

Cucumber and mint raita
SERVES 4

Refreshing and versatile, this is great with grilled food, or just a piece of pitta bread.

Grate ½ large cucumber coarsely, squeeze out excess water and place in a large bowl. Stir in 400g of yogurt, 8g of shredded mint leaves, ¾ tsp of roasted ground cumin (see page 9), and a small pinch each of caster sugar and chilli powder. Season well, taste, and adjust the seasoning. Refrigerate until ready to use.

This is lovely and creamy but light enough so as to not overpower the vegetables, which stand proud. Korma was created for the Moghul palaces, using the most expensive ingredients of the time: nuts, cream, saffron and dried fruit. Most of these are no longer so dear, except for saffron, but I do love it and always keep some in the fridge (the best place for it). If you don't have any, leave it out, the sauce will be less aromatic but still lovely. I have specified types of vegetables, but you can use almost any; I would only recommend keeping the pepper as it adds a lovely flavour.

Delicate korma with cashews and apricots

Place the onion in a saucepan and cover with boiling water. Return to the boil and simmer for around 12 minutes, or until soft. Drain. Soak 40g of the cashews and all the almonds in boiling water for 10 minutes. Drain, then peel the almonds. Blend both types of nut with the yogurt, milk, cream, coconut cream, drained onion, saffron, sugar and ground spices, adding a little water, until you have a smooth paste. Set aside.

Put the cauliflower, pepper, carrot, mushrooms and beans in a pan and add enough water to come one-quarter of the way up. Season and bring to the boil. Cover and simmer for four minutes, until just soft. Add the peas, cook for 30 seconds, then pour everything, including the cooking liquor, into a bowl.

Give the pan a wipe and place back on the heat. Add the oil and, once hot, the remaining cashews, and cook until golden. Remove and set aside. Add the cumin seeds to the pan. Once they darken, add the chillies, ginger and garlic, cook gently until the garlic smells cooked, scraping the pan if things start to stick and adding a splash of water if you're worried they might burn. Pour in the blended nut mixture and bring to the boil. Cook for five or six minutes, stirring often.

Return the vegetables with enough of their cooking liquid to give a creamy, but not thick, curry. Season to taste and add the apricots and fried cashews. Taste, adjust the seasoning and sweetness and serve.

SERVES 4

Tangerine and mint raita
SERVES 4

Lovely and refreshing with the korma.

Peel and segment 4 tangerines, removing the pithy membranes. Stir into 600g of yogurt and add 12 shredded mint leaves, a pinch of chilli powder, 1 tsp of caster sugar and salt to taste. Taste and adjust the seasoning and sugar, then refrigerate until you are ready to eat.

FOR THE KORMA

1 small onion, peeled and quartered
50g cashew nuts
40g almonds
3 rounded tbsp yogurt
200ml whole milk
4 tbsp double cream
40–50g coconut cream or creamed coconut
15 long saffron strands
1 tsp caster sugar, or to taste
½ tsp ground cardamom
½ tsp ground cinnamon
1 tsp garam masala
2 tbsp vegetable oil
1½ tsp cumin seeds
3–4 green chillies, whole but pierced with the tip of a knife
20g root ginger, peeled weight, grated
3 fat garlic cloves, peeled and grated
salt, to taste

FOR THE VEGETABLES (SEE RECIPE INTRODUCTION)

120g cauliflower, in florets
¾–1 small red pepper, in 2.5cm cubes
1 very small carrot, in 1cm half moons
100g oyster or chestnut mushrooms (choose small ones)
75g fine beans, topped, tailed and cut in three
handful of peas (I use frozen)
8 dried, ready-to-eat apricots, halved if small or quartered if large

This is a taste experience that I highly recommend. Juhu Beach is a famous stretch of sand in Mumbai. I haven't been for decades, but I remember it to be as bustling as any busy street: a throng of people to manoeuvre around, pony rides for children, blaring Bollywood music, a monotonous cacophony of hawkers... and the tempting smell of food. Pau bhaji just means bread and vegetables, but that name does no justice to this glorious recipe. It is a divine, buttery Indian vegetable mash with a thick spongy bread crisped up in butter, served with lemon wedges and red onion. You will need to buy pau bhaji masala, but this is easily available online and is a really versatile spice blend.

Juhu Beach pau bhaji

Place the pepper and cauliflower in a large, wide pan. Place on the heat, add enough water to come 1cm up the pan, bring to a boil, then reduce the heat and simmer for five minutes. Add some salt, the tomatoes, potatoes, tomato purée, paprika, 2 tsp of the pau bhaji masala, the coriander, peas and 80g of the butter.

Now you have to cook this mixture, adding water when the pan is dry. As it cooks, you need to keep mashing the whole thing (I use a potato masher) until it is all cooked and has become a lumpy purée. It will take around 30 minutes and you will keep needing to add water when it starts to catch the base of the pan. Taste; it should all seem harmonious and cooked and look lovely and creamy and mashed. Leave it on a low flame as you cook the onion.

Heat the remaining butter with the oil for the tarka in a small pan, add the onion and cook until just soft, then add the garlic and ginger and cook until the garlic is lightly golden. Add another 1 tsp of the pau bhaji masala and give it another 30 seconds, add the coriander, then pour into the vegetables. Add lemon juice to taste and a little splash of water and cook for another five minutes. Taste, adding more of the masala if you think it needs it, then adjust the seasoning and lemon juice to taste.

When ready to eat, slice the pau or burger buns in half and spread with butter. Place butter-side down in a frying pan and toast lightly, pressing down so it gets crispy and golden in places.

Serve the bread hot with the vegetables, a little bowl of finely chopped onion and the lemon wedges. Take a piece of the bread, top with some of the vegetable mixture, sprinkle over a little onion and squeeze over lemon juice to taste.

SERVES 6, CAN BE HALVED

FOR THE VEGETABLES
1 small green pepper, in roughly 1cm cubes
300g cauliflower, in small florets
salt, to taste
3 large tomatoes, chopped
2 large potatoes (500g total weight), cooked, peeled and roughly cubed
1 tbsp tomato purée
2 tsp paprika, for colour
3–4 tsp pau bhaji masala, to taste
large handful of coriander leaves, plus more to serve
large handful of peas (I use frozen)
120–140g unsalted butter, plus more for the bread (it is supposed to be buttery)
4 tsp lemon juice, or to taste

FOR THE TARKA
1 tsp vegetable oil
1 small onion, finely chopped
4 fat garlic cloves, peeled and grated
20g root ginger, peeled weight, grated
small handful of chopped coriander leaves

TO SERVE
8 pau or white burger buns
1 red onion, finely chopped
lemon wedges

Okra is a much misunderstood vegetable. Many people consider it uninteresting, or worse. But it can have a lovely texture, is flavourful and really healthy. To avoid any sliminess, the okra is cooked in a frying pan away from any liquid, then added to a lightly spiced, tangy sauce. Keeping the okra fingers intact will maintain their character and flavour. Serve with a creamy, flavourful raita (see below).

Spiced okra in tomato sauce

Heat 4 tbsp of the vegetable oil in a non-stick saucepan. Add the cumin, fennel and onion seeds and cook for 10–15 seconds, or until the cumin is aromatic. Add the onions and cook until just colouring on the edges.

Meanwhile, blend together the tomatoes and yogurt until smooth. Add to the onions with the remaining spices and some salt. Bring to the boil then simmer, stirring occasionally, until the sauce is thick and has released some oil back into the pan. Continue cooking, stirring more often, for another two to three minutes. Add 200ml of water, return to the boil, then reduce the heat and simmer gently.

Meanwhile, heat the remaining oil in a large non-stick frying pan. Add the okra and a little salt and cook, shaking the pan every now and then, for five to seven minutes, or until the okra is just soft. Add to the sauce, stir well, taste and adjust the seasoning, then simmer for another minute and serve.

SERVES 4

5 tbsp vegetable oil
½ tsp cumin seeds
½ tsp fennel seeds
½ tsp onion seeds
2 small onions, finely chopped
2 tomatoes, quartered
2 tbsp yogurt
⅓ tsp turmeric
¾ tsp garam masala
1½ tsp ground coriander
¾ tsp ground cumin
¼–½ tsp chilli powder
salt, to taste
300g okra, topped and tailed, each slit down
  its length

Carrot, cucumber and peanut raita
SERVES 4

Nutty, crunchy and lovely.
  Lightly salt 150g of coarsely grated cucumber, leave for 10 minutes, squeeze out excess water and place in a bowl. Add 1 large carrot, also coarsely grated, 3 tbsp of chopped coriander leaves, 15g of roasted peanuts, coarsely crushed, and ½ finely chopped chilli. Now stir in 250g of thick yogurt, season to taste, adding 1 tsp of caster sugar and 2 tbsp of grated fresh coconut, if you like. Heat 1 tsp of vegetable oil in a small saucepan, add ½ tsp of mustard seeds and, when the popping dies down, 6 or 7 curry leaves. Cook for another 10 seconds, then stir into the yogurt. Taste, adjust the seasoning and serve.

This is a typical Keralan curry, lighter in flavour and fresher than a North Indian curry, and quicker to make because of it. This is a great base sauce to which you can add many different vegetables: try aubergines, okra, spinach, broccoli, peas, mushrooms, chickpeas, green beans and pumpkin or squash. If you like fruity curries, some pineapple, peppers and peanuts would also be lovely (you will need to use less tamarind and perhaps add a pinch of sugar). Here I have used sweet potatoes, chickpeas and seasonal greens. Serve with rice, naan or parathas..

Keralan coconut curry

Put the sweet potatoes on to boil and cook until just done; it should take around 10 minutes.

Heat the oil in a large non-stick saucepan and add the mustard seeds. Once the popping diminishes, add the onion and green chillies and sauté for two to three minutes or until just softening, then add the ginger and garlic; sauté these gently for one minute. Add the tomatoes, salt, turmeric and ground coriander and cumin and keep sautéing for four to five minutes. Now taste; it should seem harmonious and the tomatoes should be soft but still retain their form.

Add the coconut milk and a splash of water. Bring to a gentle simmer and cook for five to seven minutes. At this point I take out the chillies as I might mistake them for spinach and inadvertently bite into one but, if you aren't using green vegetables, leave them in. Add the greens and cook for a few minutes, then add the drained sweet potatoes, the chickpeas, most of the tamarind, the garam masala and coconut cream. Taste, adjust the seasoning, adding more tamarind to taste, and serve.

SERVES 4

FOR THE VEGETABLES (SEE RECIPE INTRODUCTION FOR OTHER OPTIONS)
400g sweet potatoes, peeled, in 3cm chunks
100g shredded greens or spinach, washed
400g can chickpeas, drained and rinsed

FOR THE CURRY
4 tbsp vegetable oil
1 tsp mustard seeds
1 onion, finely chopped
3–5 green chillies, whole but pierced with the tip of a knife
25g root ginger, peeled weight, finely chopped
5 fat garlic cloves, peeled and finely chopped
2 small tomatoes, chopped
salt, to taste
½–²/₃ tsp turmeric
2 tsp ground coriander
¾–1 tsp ground cumin
400ml creamy coconut milk
½–¾ tsp tamarind paste, dissolved in a little hot water, to taste
¾ tsp garam masala, or to taste
knob of coconut cream
lots of freshly ground pepper

Rogan josh is a world-famous lamb dish from Kashmir, but has morphed quite a bit along the way... always remaining spicy, rich and very flavourful. Kashmiri dried chillies are known for the deep red colour and are mild. I serve this with Spinach and Dill Raita (see below), naan or flatbreads.

Rogan mushrooms

Roast the dried chillies in a dry pan until slightly darkened, shaking often. Break in half and shake out the seeds, then grind to a powder. Heat 4 tbsp of the oil in a large non-stick saucepan. Add the whole spices and fry for 10 seconds. Add the onions and cook until they have browned well at the edges.

Meanwhile, blend together the tomatoes, yogurt, garlic and ginger until smooth. Add to the onions with the ground spices and some salt. Cook, stirring occasionally, until the masala has completely reduced and releases oil droplets back into the pan. Continue to cook, stirring often, over a highish heat, for four to five minutes. Add 350ml of water, bring to the boil, simmer for three to four minutes, then keep warm.

Heat 1 tbsp of the remaining oil and half the butter in a large frying pan. Add half the mushrooms, sprinkle over a pinch of salt and sauté, allowing them to caramelise on the edges, for around five minutes. Repeat with the remaining oil, butter and mushrooms. As they are ready, pour the mushrooms into the sauce and stir well, then taste and adjust the seasoning. Add a little water if necessary; the sauce should be thick but not too clingy. Simmer for another three to four minutes then serve, sprinkled with the chopped coriander.

SERVES 4

2–4 dried red Kashmiri chillies
   (see recipe introduction)
6 tbsp vegetable oil
4 cloves
6 green cardamom pods
2 black cardamom pods
5cm cinnamon stick
1 mace blade
10 black peppercorns
2 small onions, finely chopped
2 large tomatoes, quartered
2 rounded tbsp yogurt
5 garlic cloves, peeled
20g root ginger, peeled weight
2 tsp ground coriander
¾ tsp ground cumin
⅓ tsp turmeric
¾ tsp garam masala, or to taste
salt, to taste
30g unsalted butter
350g assorted mushrooms (I use shiitake,
   chestnut and oyster), halved if large
handful of chopped coriander leaves

Spinach and dill raita
SERVES 4

This is silky and delicious and, somehow, children love it!
   Wilt 75g of baby spinach in a saucepan. Drain and squeeze out the excess water with your hands. Stir into 300g of yogurt, season and add ¾ tsp of roasted ground cumin (see page 9) and 10g of dill fronds, chopped. Serve chilled.

This is a classic Sindhi dish called sai bhaji. It was taught to me by my good friend Shaila and is her mother-in-law's recipe. It is so delicious that I don't think I have made a single change, which is a first! It is a proper stew, full of vegetables and so healthy, no wonder mothers insist on passing it on to their children. This is not a party dish, but one which you will cook for your family again and again; it is hearty and tangy and perfect with both Indian flatbreads and rice.

Lemony spinach and vegetable hot pot

Using a stick blender, blend together the ginger and garlic with a little water until smooth. Set aside. Again using the stick blender, blend the tomatoes until smooth. Set these aside as well.

Heat the oil in a large non-stick saucepan. Add the onion and cook until just soft. Add the blended ginger and garlic and cook until the liquid has dried up and the garlic turns lightly golden. Add the tomatoes, spices and salt and bring to the boil; simmer for five minutes.

Add the carrot, aubergine and potato and give the pan a good stir. Sprinkle over the drained lentils, but do not stir them in. Place the spinach, herbs and fenugreek on top and pour in 200ml of water. Without stirring the pan, bring to the boil, then cover and simmer on a gentle flame until yieldingly soft, around 1–1¼ hours.

Uncover and, if you like, mash the vegetables and spinach together until homogeneous (this is how the authentic recipe is made; I prefer to leave the vegetables whole). Add the lemon juice to taste and adjust the seasoning. Simmer off any excess water as the stew cooks for another 15 minutes and becomes creamy, then serve.

SERVES 5–6

20g root ginger, peeled weight
3 fat garlic cloves, peeled
4 large tomatoes, quartered
3 tbsp vegetable oil
1 large onion, chopped
2 rounded tsp ground cumin
1 tbsp ground coriander
½ tsp turmeric
1 rounded tsp garam masala
salt, to taste
1 large-ish carrot, peeled and chopped into 2cm pieces
½ large aubergine, cut into 2cm pieces
1 potato, peeled and cut into 2cm pieces
4 tbsp Bengal gram (chana dal), soaked for two hours, or as long as possible
500g baby spinach, washed
15g dill fronds or 25g coriander leaves, roughly chopped
1 tbsp dried fenugreek leaves, crumbled between your fingers
1–1½ tbsp lemon juice

This is based on a vegetarian national treasure, mirch salan, a Hyderabadi dish of fat, large green chillies in a peanut and tamarind sauce. The combination is fabulous. But I recently came across these lovely mixed baby sweet peppers at my local supermarket and decided they would be great in the dish. If you like a little more heat, find large, fat, jalapeño-type chillies and follow the recipe below, except add them to the sauce and simmer for a few minutes at the end. It is definitely a special occasion dish, but is fun to make and well worth it. The sauce also goes well with mushrooms, aubergines, okra and many other vegetables. I like to have some naan on the side to mop up all those lovely flavours.

Stuffed peppers in a peanut-tamarind sauce

Dry-roast the peanuts in a small frying pan for a minute and pour into a spice grinder. Add the sesame and cumin seeds to the pan and dry-roast gently until the sesame is golden. Pour into the spice grinder with the coconut and grind to a powder; don't worry about any chunks.

Heat 4 tbsp of the oil in a pan and add the onions; sauté until golden. Meanwhile, with a stick blender, blend the ginger and garlic with a little water until smooth. Separately, blend the tomatoes until smooth. Add the ginger and garlic to the onions and sauté until the garlic colours. Add the tomatoes, ground spices and salt. Bring to the boil and cook for 10–15 minutes, until the masala releases oil back into the pan. Brown this paste, over a highish heat, for three to four minutes, then stir in the ground nut mixture. Add 400ml of water, return to the boil and simmer for eight minutes. Add most of the tamarind, then adjust the seasoning and tamarind. It should be a slightly chunky, creamy curry, neither watery nor too thick.

For the stuffing, heat 1 tbsp of the remaining oil in a large non-stick frying pan. Add the onion and cook until soft, add the turmeric and, after a beat, the potato, cumin and salt to taste; cook for two minutes. Add the lemon juice, mix, adjust the seasoning and place in a bowl to cool. Give it a good mash if it is lumpy. Wipe the pan. Slit the peppers lengthways so you can open them, then stuff them. Do not overstuff.

Cook the peppers in two batches: in 1 tbsp of the remaining oil for each batch, add half the mustard seeds and reduce the heat. Once the popping dies down, add half the curry leaves and peppers. Stir for 20 seconds and season lightly. Then add a splash of hot water, cover and steam for 10 minutes or until the peppers are soft; they will have lightly charred in places. Shake gently every so often. Keep warm while you repeat with the next batch.

Place the peppers on warmed plates. Spoon the sauce over and sprinkle with coconut, or peanuts and chopped coriander. Serve hot.

SERVES 6

70g raw peanuts, skins rubbed off if there are any, plus more to serve (optional)
2 tbsp sesame seeds
1 tbsp cumin seeds
1 rounded tbsp desiccated coconut, plus more to serve (optional)
7 tbsp vegetable oil
2 onions, finely chopped
20g root ginger, peeled weight
4 large garlic cloves, peeled
2 tomatoes, quartered
1 rounded tbsp ground coriander
1½ tsp garam masala
½ tsp turmeric
¼–½ tsp chilli powder, or to taste
salt, to taste
½–¾ tsp tamarind paste, dissolved in 3 tbsp boiling water, or to taste
12 baby mixed peppers
¾ tsp mustard seeds
10 curry leaves
small fistful of chopped coriander leaves, to serve (optional)

FOR THE STUFFING
½ onion, finely chopped
²⁄₃ tsp turmeric
450g potatoes, boiled or microwaved, peeled and coarsely mashed
1 rounded tsp cumin seeds
1½–2 tsp lemon juice

I don't know anyone who doesn't love a pie; they are comforting and homey and also special enough for when you have friends around. This pie doesn't need any more than a salad on the side. I love the rustic cobbler topping, it is really quick and simple, but you can also cover the pie with puff pastry if you prefer. You can serve this in a large dish, or individual dishes. I roast the squash here rather than cooking it in the curry, only because it is easier than cutting raw squash into pieces!

Autumnal squash, butterbean and mushroom cobbler

Preheat the oven to 200°C/400°F/gas mark 6. Halve the squash, remove any fibres and seeds, but leave the skin on. Place it in a roasting tin and cook until soft, around 30 minutes. Cut into 2.5cm squares, removing the skin if you want.

Meanwhile, heat the oil in a large saucepan until hot. Add the onion and cook until soft and colouring at the edges. Add the ginger and garlic and cook until the garlic just starts to colour. Add the tomatoes, spices and seasoning and cook down until the sauce has thickened and has released oil back into the pan.

Add the mushrooms, cover and cook for another two to three minutes. Pour in 200ml of water and add the beans, squash and spinach and return to the boil. Cook for two to three minutes. Add the cream and milk, taste – making sure you taste both squash and sauce – and adjust the seasoning. Stir in the tomato purée if you feel the tomatoes are lacking flavour or colour. By now the sauce should be thick and cling to the vegetables. Spoon into a large pie dish, or six individual dishes.

Make the cobbler topping. Place the flour and salt in a large bowl, add the butter and rub between your fingers until you have a sandy texture. Make a well in the middle, add half the egg and most of the milk and bring together with a fork to a very soft dough. Turn out on to a flour-dusted work surface and lightly bring together. Pat out until it is about 1cm thick and, using a pastry cutter, cut out six rounds. (I use large cutters and make the rounds big enough to cover the filling with just a little showing at the sides.)

Place the cobbler rounds on the pie filling, brush with the remaining beaten egg, sprinkle over some sea salt and bake on the middle shelf of the oven until the cobbler topping has turned a lovely deep golden brown, 20–25 minutes. Serve.

SERVES 5–6

FOR THE PIE FILLING
400g squash (I like butternut, hubbard
  or acorn)
4 tbsp vegetable oil
1 onion, chopped
20g root ginger, peeled weight, grated
3 large garlic cloves, peeled and grated
3 tomatoes, quartered
¾ tsp turmeric
½–1 tsp chilli powder
2 tsp ground coriander
½ tsp garam masala
salt, to taste
good pinch of freshly ground black pepper
9–10 large chestnut mushrooms,
  thickly sliced
400g can butterbeans, drained and rinsed
100g baby spinach
6 tbsp double cream
50ml whole milk
½–1 tbsp tomato purée (optional)

FOR THE COBBLER TOPPING
175g self-raising flour, sifted,
  plus more to dust
⅓ tsp salt
70g unsalted butter, cut into smallish pieces
2 eggs, beaten
55–65ml whole milk
a few sea salt flakes

I love sweetcorn in most guises, but few dishes are as delicious as this. The cobs are enrobed in a tangy, tomato-based curry laced with crushed roasted peanuts, adding texture and flavour. The result is absolutely delicious and the dish easy to make. I normally eat the cobs with my fingers and mop up the sauce with Indian breads but, if that feels awkward, use sweetcorn kernels instead of cobs and eat the dish with a knife and fork.

Sweetcorn cobs in tangy peanut masala

Heat the oil in a large non-stick saucepan. Add the cumin seeds, follow with the onion and sauté until golden.

Meanwhile, blend together the tomatoes, ginger and garlic until smooth. Add to the onion with the ground spices. Cook until the masala has completely reduced and released oil back into the pan. Stir-fry for three to four minutes to intensify the flavours.

Meanwhile, bring a large pot of water to the boil and add your corn cobs. Return to the boil and cook for 10 minutes, or until the kernels are just tender. Drain and, when cool enough to handle, cut each cob into four with a heavy knife (be very careful).

Returning to the masala, add the peanuts with 600ml of water and bring to the boil, then reduce the heat and simmer for five minutes. Add the corn cobs, cover and simmer for another five to seven minutes or until the sauce has thickened and there is a little oil on the surface.

Taste and adjust the seasoning, adding coriander leaves and lemon juice to taste. The sauce will taste different when eaten with the sweetcorn so, if you are not sure, serve the dish with lemon wedges on the side.

SERVES 4

4 tbsp vegetable oil
1½ tsp cumin seeds
1 red onion, finely chopped
5 tomatoes
20g root ginger, peeled weight
4 large garlic cloves, peeled
2 rounded tsp ground coriander
⅓ tsp turmeric
1½ tsp garam masala
¾ tsp chilli powder, to taste
4 small sweetcorn cobs
150g roasted peanuts, coarsely crushed
salt, to taste
handful of coriander leaves
lemon juice, to taste (I add around 1–1½ tbsp because I like the tang), plus lemon wedges to serve (optional)

This is a tomato-based curry where the vegetables take centre stage, retaining their own textures and flavours. You really can make a jhalfrezi with any vegetables as long as you use the same volume; I have listed a few options just to give you some ideas. Look for a good mix of colours, shapes and textures. If you can find baby vegetables, it will make this even more special. Only use pomegranate seeds if they are ripe, otherwise they add too much sourness. I like this quite spicy, so like to add crushed chillies at the end, but I leave that up to you and your palate. Serve with naan.

Vegetable jhalfrezi with pomegranates

Using a stick blender, blend the tomatoes until smooth. Heat the oil in a large non-stick saucepan. Add the grated ginger and garlic and cook, stirring often, until the garlic is cooked and starts to colour, around one minute. Add the green chillies, tomatoes, ground coriander, garam masala and salt. Bring to the boil and allow to simmer until the tomatoes have completely reduced and the sauce releases oil on the base of the pan. Taste; it should seem harmonious.

Meanwhile, cook your chosen vegetables. Bring a pot of water to the boil and salt lightly. Add your vegetables in order of how long they take to cook. I add the starchier vegetables first (here the potatoes, carrots and squash), then follow five minutes later with the aubergines and courgettes, then one to two minutes later with the beans and peas. Cook until they are ready, another two minutes or so. Check as you cook. Drain, but reserve the cooking water.

When ready to serve, add the red pepper strips, ginger julienne, fenugreek leaves and 150ml of the vegetable cooking liquor to the sauce and return to a boil. Taste and adjust the seasoning, adding the crushed chilli, if using. Add the vegetables and stir well to coat them in the light tomato sauce. Splash in a little water if the sauce is too thick; it should be of coating consistency. Ladle into a warmed serving dish, spoon over the cream in a circular pattern, sprinkle the pomegranate powder over the cream so you can see it and then do the same with the pomegranate seeds, if using. Serve.

SERVES 4

FOR THE SAUCE

2 large ripe tomatoes, quartered
5 tbsp vegetable oil, or a mix of unsalted butter and oil
15g root ginger, peeled weight, half grated, half sliced into fine julienne
4 fat garlic cloves, peeled and grated
4–5 green chillies, whole but pierced with the tip of a knife
2 rounded tsp ground coriander
1 tsp garam masala
salt, to taste
½ small red pepper, finely sliced
2 tsp dried fenugreek leaves, crushed
¼ tsp crushed red chillies (optional)
2 tbsp single cream (optional)
good pinch of dried pomegranate powder (optional)
handful of pomegranate seeds (optional)

FOR THE VEGETABLES (YOU NEED 3 HANDFULS OF PREPARED VEGETABLES)

fingerling or baby potatoes, cooked, peeled, then halved or quartered lengthways
carrots or parsnips, peeled, halved lengthways, then sliced at an angle
wedge of butternut squash or pumpkin, peeled, cut into wedges
Japanese aubergines, quartered lengthways (leave the stalk on)
courgettes, sliced at an angle
broad beans, sugar snap peas, French beans or mangetout (all trimmed, and French beans halved)

This is a lovely delicate, pale curry where you can taste all the vegetables but also the delicate mint and pistachios. You can use whichever vegetables you prefer, these are just a few I like to use. I tend to cook my vegetables before adding them to a sauce, so both sauce and vegetables retain their own characters. Serve with naan, paratha or a pilaf.

Creamy pistachio curry

Bring a pot of water to the boil and salt lightly. Add your vegetables in order of how long they take to cook. I add the starchier vegetables first (here the squash), then follow five minutes later with the cauliflower, then one to two minutes later with the broccoli and mangetout. Cook until they are ready, another two minutes or so. Check as you cook. Drain, but reserve the cooking water.

Meanwhile, soak the pistachios for five minutes in boiling water Remove the skins; they peel off easily when rubbed in a clean tea towel. Roughly chop one-third of the nuts. Blend together the rest of the pistachios until smooth, adding a little water to help.

Heat the oil in a large non-stick saucepan; add the cloves, cardamom, cassia and caraway seeds. Follow after 20 seconds with the onion and green chillies and cook until the onion is golden on the edges. Add the ginger and garlic and sauté gently for one to two minutes, or until the garlic is just golden.

Add the ground cumin and coriander and the yogurt and bring to the boil, stirring constantly. Continue to cook, stirring, until the masala thickens and releases oil back into the pan, around five to eight minutes. Taste; it should seem harmonious. If not, cook for another couple of minutes.

Add the blanched vegetables, some of their cooking water, the pepper, cream and both blended and chopped pistachios. Cook for another two or three minutes for everything to come together. The sauce should be creamy and not too thick, so add water if necessary. Check the seasoning, adjust as necessary, crumble over the dried mint, then serve.

SERVES 4

FOR THE VEGETABLES (AROUND 350G, USE WHICHEVER YOU PREFER)
salt
100g butternut squash, cut into 3–4cm cubes (or sweet potato or carrots)
100g cauliflower, cut into 3–4cm florets
100g broccoli, cut into 3–4cm florets
50g mangetout, trimmed (or other beans or peas)

FOR THE CURRY
60g pistachio nuts
4 tbsp vegetable oil
6 cloves
6 green cardamom pods
5cm cassia bark or cinnamon stick
1 tsp caraway seeds
1 small-ish onion, finely chopped
1–2 green chillies, whole but pierced with the tip of a knife
20g root ginger, peeled weight, grated
4 fat garlic cloves, peeled and grated
1¼ tsp ground cumin
2 tsp ground coriander
5 tbsp yogurt
large pinch of freshly ground black pepper
5 tbsp single cream
1 tbsp good-quality dried mint, crumbled between your fingers, or to taste

CHEESE, PULSES
AND EGGS

Dhansak is a fantastic dish from the Parsi community, made from lentils and vegetables. If you are a fan of dhansak, it might be worth buying the ready-made masala available in most Indian shops (even Parsis use it), though I've given my own recipe here (see below). I like to serve this with sim rice. The traditional vegetables used are pumpkin, aubergine and potatoes, but I often seasonal greens for a one-pot meal (blanch green vegetables before using). Starchy ve as sweet potato, turnips and so on can be added straight to the lentils.

Parsi dhansak

Place the pigeon peas and both types of lentil in a bowl and wash in several changes of water, until the water runs clear.

Heat the oil in a large saucepan. Add the onion and sauté until just browned on the edges. Add the ginger and garlic and sauté gently for one to two minutes. Add the lentils, tomato, salt and turmeric and stir for a few minutes. Pour in enough water to cover by 5cm and bring to the boil, then reduce the heat, cover and simmer for 25–30 minutes, or until the lentils are soft. Stir occasionally, as the lentils will settle on the bottom of the pan, and add water from the kettle as necessary.

Blend until smooth (I plunge my stick blender into the pot). Add the vegetables with a good splash of water and cook for five minutes. Now add the tamarind, sugar, dhansak masala and fenugreek and cook for another five minutes, or until the vegetables are just soft. Taste, adjust the seasoning, sugar and tamarind, stir in the coriander and serve.

SERVES 4–6, CAN BE HALVED

100g split pigeon peas (toor dal)
50g red lentils (masoor dal)
50g yellow lentils (mung dal)
4 tbsp vegetable oil
1 onion, sliced
15g root ginger, peeled weight, roughly sliced
4 fat garlic cloves, peeled and roughly sliced
1 tomato, roughly chopped
salt, to taste
⅓ tsp turmeric
¾–1 tsp tamarind paste, dissolved in a little water, or to taste
2–2½ tsp caster sugar, or to taste
4 tbsp My Dhansak Masala (see below left), or to taste
2 tsp dried fenugreek leaves, crushed between your fingers
large handful of chopped coriander leaves

VEGETABLES I HAVE USED (FOR OTHER OPTIONS SEE ABOVE):
125g squash or sweet potatoes, in 2.5cm cubes
125g Japanese aubergines, topped, tailed and cut across into halves or thirds

My dhansak masala

Place 2 tbsp of coriander seeds, 1cm of cinnamon stick, 3 cloves and 1 star anise in a dry frying pan and place over a medium heat, shaking to brown the spices evenly. After 30 seconds, add 1½ tsp of cumin seeds and ½ tsp each of caraway, mustard and fenugreek seeds and roast, shaking the pan often, until the fenugreek and cumin seeds darken, another 30–40 seconds or so. Tip into a spice or coffee grinder, add 8 black peppercorns, ¼ tsp of freshly grated nutmeg and 1–2 dried chillies. Grind until smooth. Store in a jar in a cool, dark place. This should make enough for the recipe above, allowing for more to be added if you want it.

The lentil curry I eat more than any other. You won't find it on restaurant menus – it is lighter and thinner than the familiar versions – but you can taste the lentils and all the ...rs. I eat it with Indian flatbread and a simple, dry ... ...ou can also fry the onions, ginger, garlic a... ... oil instead of adding them straight to the lent... ... it this way.

Easy everyday lentil curry

Place both types of lentil in a bowl and wash in several changes of water, until the water runs clear. Now place them in a large saucepan with water to cover by 5cm and bring to the boil. Skim the surface of any scum. Add the onion, ginger, garlic, chillies, tomatoes, turmeric and seasoning. Return to the boil, reduce the heat, then simmer, partially covered, until the lentils are cooked and the curry starts to look homogeneous, around 40 minutes.

Heat the ghee or butter in a very small saucepan and allow it to pool on one side. Add the cumin seeds and asafoetida. Once the seeds darken, add the garam masala and ground coriander and take off the heat. Pour into the lentils, add the chopped coriander and serve.

SERVES 4

125g yellow lentils (mung dal), washed well
75g red lentils (masoor dal), washed well
½ onion, finely chopped
10g root ginger, peeled weight,
  finely chopped
2 garlic cloves, peeled and finely chopped
2–4 green chillies, whole but pierced with the
  tip of a knife
2 tomatoes, chopped
½ tsp turmeric
salt, to taste
1½–2 tbsp ghee or unsalted butter
2 rounded tsp cumin seeds
⅛ tsp, or a small pinch, asafoetida
½ tsp garam masala
¾ tsp ground coriander
handful of chopped coriander leaves

A classic North Indian dish, this can be dramatic looking, as the yellow lentils stand out from the smaller black pulses. Most importantly, it is luscious and delicious. Once the lentils soften, the more you stir them the creamier they become. Lentils and butter go really well together, so I do recommend you add a little butter at the end before serving. This is great with rice or Indian breads.

Bengal tiger lentil curry

Using a stick blender, blend the 10g chunk of ginger and the garlic with a little water until smooth. Separately blend the tomatoes until smooth. Set both aside. Place both types of lentil in a bowl and wash in several changes of water, until the water runs clear. Now tip them into a large pot, pour in enough water to cover by 7.5cm and bring to the boil. Skim any scum from the surface. Add the turmeric and some salt. Cook, partially covered, giving an occasional stir, until the lentils have softened and are starting to look homogeneous with the water. (Stir more often as they become tender.)

After about 40 minutes, start to make the tarka, but remember to keep giving the lentils a stir. Heat the oil or ghee in a small non-stick saucepan. Add the cumin seeds and, once they sizzle and darken, add the onion and cook until colouring at the edges. Add the ginger and garlic paste and cook until the extra moisture has evaporated and the garlic is starting to colour. Add the tomatoes and remaining ground spices and cook down for 10–15 minutes, until the masala releases oil.

Pour the tarka into the lentils with the ginger julienne, adding water from the kettle if it seems too thick. Make sure the whole thing looks like a lovely unctuous mass (if not, cook a little longer, adding water if necessary) then taste and adjust the seasoning. Stir in the chopped coriander and butter, if using, and serve.

SERVES 4–5

20g root ginger, peeled weight,
   half of it sliced into fine julienne
4 garlic cloves, peeled
4 small-ish tomatoes, quartered
175g Bengal gram (chana dal)
75g split black gram (dhuli hui ma dal)
½ tsp turmeric
salt, to taste
4 tbsp vegetable oil, or half oil, half ghee
2 tsp cumin seeds
1 large-ish onion, finely chopped
2 tsp ground coriander
1 tsp ground cumin
¾ tsp garam masala
¼–½ tsp chilli powder
handful of chopped coriander leaves
10–20g unsalted butter, to serve (optional,
   see recipe introduction)

The vegetarian version of the much-loved chicken dish, this is absolutely delicious, with a wonderful creamy tomato sauce and a few key spices that work beautifully with the paneer. It is definitely for special occasions, as it has a few steps and is unapologetically creamy. Before you serve it up, please take a minute to balance your sauce for sweetness and tartness, which will vary with the tomatoes. Adjust and taste until you are happy with the balance. Serve with naan or paratha.

Paneer tikka masala

Blend together the ingredients for the tikka marinade until smooth, scrape into a bowl, add the paneer and stir to coat.

With a stick blender, blend the tomatoes until smooth. Heat the oil and half the butter in a large non-stick saucepan. Add the whole spices and cook for 10 seconds before adding the ginger and garlic; cook gently until starting to colour. Add the tomatoes and tomato purée and cook down until the resulting paste releases oil, around 20 minutes. Now, over a medium-low flame, 'brown' this paste, stirring often, until it darkens considerably, around eight to 10 minutes. Add 250ml of water, bring to the boil, then pass through a sieve, pressing down on the solids with the back of a spoon until all you have left are fibre and spices; throw these away.

Heat the grill on its highest setting. Place the paneer on a foil-lined tray and grill for eight to 10 minutes, turning once, or until the edges are lightly charred. Remove from the oven.

Heat the remaining butter and add the green chillies. Add the tomato sauce, powdered spices, salt, sugar and a good splash of water and simmer for two or three minutes. Add the paneer and simmer for another five to six minutes. Add the cream and simmer, shaking the pan gently, until the sauce is lovely and creamy, around two or three minutes. You may need to add a little more water to get the consistency of single cream. Taste and adjust the balance by adding more salt, sugar or cream as necessary (cream will lessen any overt acidity from under-ripe tomatoes). Serve and wait for the applause.

SERVES 4–6

FOR THE TIKKA MARINADE

10g root ginger, peeled weight
2 fat garlic cloves, peeled
2 tbsp lemon juice
150g Greek yogurt
1 rounded tsp chilli powder
1 rounded tsp ground cumin
1 rounded tsp garam masala
1 rounded tsp paprika
salt, to taste
3 tbsp vegetable oil

FOR THE REST

400g paneer (preferably homemade, see page 9), in 3–4cm cubes
500g vine tomatoes, quartered
1 tbsp vegetable oil
60g unsalted butter
1 black cardamom pod
6 green cardamom pods
5cm cinnamon stick
4 cloves
20g root ginger, peeled weight, grated
4 garlic cloves, grated
1 tbsp tomato purée
2–4 small green chillies, whole but pierced with the tip of a knife
½ tsp garam masala
1 tsp paprika, or enough to get a good colour
1½ rounded tsp dried fenugreek leaves, crushed with your fingers
salt, to taste
1¼–1½ tsp caster sugar, or to taste
60–80ml single cream, or to taste

I was introduced to this delicious sweet-and-sour lentil dish at a friend's house in Mumbai. It quickly became a firm favourite and they made it for me every trip. Here, I have added dumplings with a vibrant pea and coconut filling to freshen the lentils and make it more elegant, but you can leave them out and just add some diamond-shaped pieces of roti to the lentils, or even leave the lentils as they are. This quite soupy dish is normally served as a stand-alone meal. Cocum is a fruit that grows on tropical trees in parts of India; the dark purple flesh is dried. It adds a lovely sourness and tastes absolutely delicious. If you don't have any, balance the sourness to taste with the tamarind.

Green pea and coconut dumplings in Gujarati lentil curry

Put the pigeon peas in a saucepan and pour in enough water to cover by 5cm. Bring to the boil, then add salt and the turmeric and cook, partially covered, for 30 minutes, or until soft, skimming any scum from the surface. Using a stick blender, blend to a smooth purée.

Meanwhile, mix all the ingredients for the dough, adding 45ml of water and a pinch of salt. Knead well until soft and elastic. Set aside, covered with a damp piece of kitchen paper.

For the filling, pour boiling water over the peas and leave for five minutes, then drain and squeeze out excess water. Put the peas into a bowl. Heat the ghee in a small pan and add the mustard seeds. Once they have popped, pour into the peas with the remaining filling ingredients; mash them with a fork, season to taste and set aside.

Add the tomato, sugar, ginger, chilli powder, peanuts and cocum (if using) to the lentils. Then heat the ghee in a small saucepan; add the asafoetida and whole spices and, once the popping starts to subside, stir in the ground coriander and curry leaves. Cook for another two to three seconds, then pour into the lentils. Return to the boil, cover and simmer for 15 minutes.

Meanwhile make the dumplings. Roll the dough into a rope and cut into eight equal pieces. Take one and use a little extra flour to help you roll it out into a very thin 7.5cm disc. Fill with 1 tbsp of filling and close like a pasty, folding over and pinching the seam. Repeat with the rest.

Pour enough boiling water into the lentils so they have a thin consistency. Add most of the tamarind, taste and adjust the salt, sugar and tamarind to taste. Add the dumplings to the curry and return to the boil, then reduce the heat and simmer gently for 10 minutes. Serve in warmed soup bowls with two dumplings each.

SERVES 4

FOR THE LENTIL CURRY
200g split pigeon peas (toor dal), well washed
salt, to taste
½ tsp turmeric
1 large-ish tomato, chopped
2 tbsp jaggery or brown sugar, or to taste
15g root ginger, peeled weight, grated
¼–½ tsp chilli powder
2 tbsp dry roasted peanuts, coarsely crushed (optional)
8 dried cocum, soaked (optional)
2 tbsp ghee
¼ tsp asafoetida
4 cloves
7.5cm cinnamon stick
½ tsp each mustard and cumin seeds
¼ tsp fenugreek seeds
1 tsp ground coriander
10 curry leaves
1 tsp tamarind paste, dissolved in a little hot water, or to taste

FOR THE DOUGH
65g chapati flour, plus more to dust
¼ tsp each turmeric and carom seeds
1 tbsp vegetable oil

FOR THE FILLING
130g frozen peas
1 rounded tsp ghee
⅓ tsp mustard seeds
2 rounded tbsp desiccated coconut
10g root ginger, peeled weight, grated
small handful of chopped coriander leaves

This is a North Indian classic. Normally the cubes of paneer are lightly fried before being added to the sauce – which changes their texture and flavour and crisps their sides – but adding 'raw' paneer, as I do here, makes it lighter and creamier. If you are making this dish earlier in the day for supper, or even a day before, then fry the paneer, as it keeps its shape better. Serve with naan or roti.

Paneer and pea curry

Heat the oil in a large non-stick saucepan, add the whole spices and cook for 20 seconds. Add the onions and sauté gently until they are a deep golden brown. Add the garlic and cook for one or two minutes, or until the garlic smells cooked.

Meanwhile, blend together the tomatoes and ginger with a good splash of water until smooth. Add to the pot with the ground spices and salt. Bring to the boil, then reduce the heat to a simmer and cook down until it is a thick paste, stirring every so often in the beginning and then more as the paste thickens. Taste; it should seem harmonious with no raw elements to it.

Add the peas and tomato purée and cook for a minute or two, then pour in 500ml of water and bring to a boil. Add the paneer, return to the boil, then reduce the heat and simmer for five to six minutes. Stir in the coriander leaves and cream. Taste and adjust the seasoning, adding the sugar if it seems acidic, as well as a little extra boiling water if the curry looks too thick, then serve.

SERVES 4–6

5 tbsp vegetable oil (or half oil and half ghee, or unsalted butter, for more flavour)
4 dried or 2 fresh bay leaves
4 black cardamom pods
10 black peppercorns
2 small onions, finely chopped
3 large garlic cloves, peeled and finely chopped
4 large tomatoes, quartered
20g root ginger, peeled weight
2 tsp ground coriander
½ tsp chilli powder
½ tsp turmeric
1 tsp garam masala
salt, to taste
200g frozen peas
1½ tbsp tomato purée (or more if your tomatoes aren't great)
300g paneer (preferably homemade, see page 9), in 2cm cubes
good handful of chopped coriander leaves
3–4 tbsp double cream
pinch of caster sugar (optional)

This dish, khao sway, came to India during the Second World War and has grown in popularity over the years. Once a simple recipe, it is now a dinner party favourite. I have added a few vegetables and some eggs, but you can vary the accompaniments to your own taste. The curry is normally served with coriander, chillies, fried garlic and lemons on the side, so guests add what they like. To shred the potato for the potato straws, I use the slicer part of my box grater, then finely slice the paper-thin rounds into long, fine julienne; it works beautifully.

Burmese-style egg, vegetable and noodle coconut curry

Heat the oil for the curry in a large non-stick saucepan. Add the fenugreek and fry until browned, then the onion. Cook over a high heat until caramelised at the edges. Meanwhile, blend the tomato, ginger and garlic with water until smooth. Add the gram flour to the onion and sauté over a medium flame for one minute, scraping the pan often.

Add the tomato mixture, all the spices and salt. Give it a good stir and cook until it thickens considerably, 12–15 minutes over a medium-low flame, stirring often. Remove and reserve the dried chillies, add a splash of water and blend until smooth. Pour back into the rinsed-out pan and return the chillies. Add the coconut milk and 150ml of water and simmer for five minutes. Now add the coconut cream, lemon juice and sugar. The sauce should be creamy but not too thick.

Toss the potato straws in the salt in a bowl. Gently heat 3.5cm of oil in a saucepan (the wider the pan the more you can do at once). When the oil is medium-hot, squeeze out as much water as you can from the potatoes and add one or two large handfuls to the oil. Do not overcrowd the pan. Fry for five to six minutes, breaking up tangled straws, until lightly golden and crispy. Remove with a slotted spoon and drain on kitchen paper. Repeat to cook all the straws.

Meanwhile, boil the eggs for eight minutes. Heat 1 tbsp of the vegetable oil in a large non-stick frying pan, add the okra, season and stir for a few minutes, then cover and cook until soft (three to four minutes). Remove. Heat another 1 tbsp of oil in the pan and add the mushrooms, season and fry until golden and crisp on the edges.

Cook the noodles according to the packet instructions and mound in the centre of deep plates. Pour the sauce over and arrange the eggs, okra and mushrooms around. Sprinkle with chopped coriander, peanuts and potato straws. Serve with lemon wedges and sliced chillies.

SERVES 4

FOR THE COCONUT CURRY
4–5 tbsp vegetable oil
¼ tsp fenugreek seeds
1 large onion, sliced
1 large-ish tomato, quartered
20g root ginger, peeled weight
5 garlic cloves, peeled
1 rounded tbsp gram (chickpea) flour
2–3 dried red chillies
½ tsp turmeric
1 tbsp ground coriander
1½ tsp ground cumin
1½ tsp garam masala, or to taste
salt, to taste
400ml coconut milk
50g coconut cream
2–3 tsp lemon juice, or to taste
good pinch of caster sugar (optional)

FOR THE POTATO STRAWS (SALLI)
1 potato, shredded (see recipe introduction)
⅓ tsp salt
vegetable oil, to deep-fry

FOR THE REST
4–6 eggs
2 tbsp vegetable oil
150g whole okra, or 1 small aubergine, sliced
8–12 large oyster mushrooms
220g egg noodles (I like wide, flat noodles)
handful of chopped coriander leaves
4 tbsp salted and roasted peanuts
lemon wedges, to serve
1–2 large red chillies, sliced, to serve

Black-eyed beans are absolutely delicious, delicate but with a distinctive flavour that I prefer to all other beans. They have been part of the Indian diet for thousands of years but I have never seen them on a restaurant menu, which is a pity as they make a lovely, light curry. This recipe is inspired by the West Coast of India. If you don't love coconut, you can make this without (add water instead, leave out the tamarind and keep the curry quite thick). Serve with Indian bread or a rice pilaf, or plain boiled rice.

Black-eyed bean and coconut curry

Drain the soaked beans, tip into a large saucepan and add fresh water to come 5cm above the level of the beans. Bring to the boil, cover and cook until just soft, around 45 minutes. Salt the beans lightly about 30 minutes into cooking. Remove from the heat and drain, reserving 250–300ml of the cooking water.

Heat the oil in a non-stick saucepan. Add the mustard seeds and, once they pop, add the curry leaves and cook for another few seconds. Add the onion and green chillies and cook until the onion is golden brown on the edges.

Meanwhile, blend together the garlic, ginger and tomato until smooth. Add to the cooked onions with the ground cumin and coriander, chilli powder and a splash of water, and season. Cook over a medium-high heat until completely reduced, stirring occasionally to start with, then more as the moisture dries up. Once the masala has released oil back into the pan and tastes harmonious, add the cooked dried beans (or canned beans, if using) and the reserved cooking liquid, or 250–300ml of water if using canned beans. Bring to the boil and cook until all the moisture in the pot has evaporated, stirring occasionally.

Add the coconut milk and enough water to make a creamy curry (around 250ml), return to a boil and simmer for five minutes for the whole thing to come together. Stir in the tamarind paste and garam masala, adjust the seasoning and serve sprinkled with the coriander.

SERVES 4–5

200g dried black-eyed beans, washed well and soaked overnight (or 2 x 400g cans, drained and rinsed well)
salt, to taste
3 tbsp vegetable oil
1 tsp mustard seeds
10 curry leaves
1 small-ish onion, finely chopped
2 green chillies, whole but pierced with the tip of a knife
3 fat garlic cloves, peeled
20g root ginger, peeled weight
1 large-ish tomato, quartered
1 tsp ground cumin
1 tsp ground coriander
1/8–1/4 tsp chilli powder, or to taste
240ml coconut milk
1/3–1/2 tsp tamarind paste, or to taste
1/2–3/4 tsp garam masala, or to taste
handful of chopped coriander leaves

Forgot to soak overnight?

Bring the beans and enough water to cover to the boil, then boil for one minute. Remove from the heat, cover tightly, and let stand for one hour. Drain well and cook as above.

A vegetarian Indian take on the British classic pie. I cook Quorn mince quite often, as my daughter and I love it. Sometimes it's eaten with Indian breads, other times with buttered bread, and here it is topped with creamy, cheesy mashed potatoes to make a substantial, delicious one-pot meal. You can also omit the Quorn and make the dish with some Puy lentils or a mixture of lentils and beans, if you prefer. Whichever way you make this, it is delicious and very satisfying. I normally serve greens on the side.

Luscious spiced cottage pie

Heat the vegetable oil and add the onion, cardamom pods and bay leaves. Cook until the onion is starting to colour at the edges. Preheat the oven to 200°C/400°F/gas mark 6.

Using a stick blender, blend the chunk of ginger and the garlic with a little water until smooth. Separately blend the tomatoes until smooth. Add the ginger and garlic paste to the onion and cook gently. Once the garlic has started to colour, add the tomatoes, tomato purée and the remaining spices and seasoning. Cook over a medium-high flame, stirring occasionally, until the masala has thickened, looks like a tomato paste and releases oil back into the pan. Taste, it should be harmonious with no sharp notes. Add the mince and stir-fry for three to four minutes. Now pour in 400ml of water, bring to the boil, then reduce the heat and simmer until most of the liquid has been absorbed. Add the peas after three minutes. Taste and adjust the seasoning, making sure you have added a good pinch of black pepper, and add lemon juice if it needs it. Stir in the chopped coriander and turn off the heat.

Meanwhile, place the potatoes in a pan of cold water, bring to the boil and cook until just tender to the point of a knife. Drain well and allow them to dry off in the pan for a minute. Using a potato ricer or masher, mash well, add the butter, milk and cheese and mash and stir until amalgamated; I like mine a little lumpy. Season to taste, adding lots of black pepper.

Spoon the mince evenly into an ovenproof, table-ready dish. Pipe or spoon on the mash to cover, decorate as you like (not at all, or with the tines of a fork). If you would like a golden finish, dot the surface all over with small cubes of butter. Place in the middle of the oven and bake for 30 minutes, or until golden. Serve hot.

SERVES 4 GENEROUSLY

FOR THE FILLING

3 tbsp vegetable oil
1 onion, finely chopped
3 black cardamom pods
2 bay leaves
20g root ginger, peeled weight,
    10g of it sliced into fine julienne
3 garlic cloves, peeled
2 tomatoes, quartered
1 tbsp tomato purée, or to taste
2 tsp ground coriander
¼–½ tsp chilli powder, or to taste
1 tsp garam masala
1 tsp ground cumin
salt, to taste
freshly ground black pepper, to taste
350g Quorn (or other vegetarian mince)
2 small handfuls of frozen peas
lemon juice, to taste
large handful of chopped coriander leaves

FOR THE TOPPING

600g floury potatoes, peeled and cut in
    large pieces
60g unsalted butter, plus more
    to cook (optional)
65–80ml whole milk
50–60g mature cheddar cheese

One of our staple Sunday lunches, this is a Punjabi stalwart, loved by meat-eaters and vegetarians alike. It seems to be a dish that Indians across the subcontinent appreciate, regardless of their own regional cuisine, and one I get plenty of requests for online. So here it is. It might not look great on paper, but it is wonderful on the plate. I really prefer dried kidney beans here, as they have more flavour and a better texture. This does mean overnight soaking and a long cook in the morning, but aside from some forethought it's no harder than using canned, and is more rewarding. (When I tested the recipe with canned beans, the sauce needed some help, see below.) Serve with plain basmati rice.

Sunday lunch kidney bean curry

Drain the soaked beans and tip them into a large saucepan. Cover with fresh water and bring to the boil. Boil hard for 10 minutes, then reduce the heat to a lively simmer and cook for 1½ to 1¾ hours. After they have been cooking for 1¼ hours, blend the onion with a little water until smooth. Separately blend the ginger and garlic in the same way.

Heat the oil in a large non-stick frying pan, add the onion paste and cook until really well browned (it should look like chocolate), stirring often as it starts to brown. Add the ginger and garlic paste and cook until you can smell the garlic is cooked, around one minute after the water has dried up. Meanwhile, blend the tomatoes with a stick blender until smooth and add them to the pan with the spices and seasoning. Cook this on a medium-low flame until it is completely cooked through and is very thick, resembling tomato purée, around 25 minutes.

Drain the cooked kidney beans and reserve the cooking liquor. Add the beans to the tomato sauce and stir for one minute, then pour in 450ml of the bean cooking liquor, bring to the boil, reduce the heat and simmer for five minutes. Throw in the chopped coriander, taste, adjust the seasoning and serve.

SERVES 3–4

200g dried kidney beans, washed well and
    soaked overnight (if you have to use
    canned beans, see below)
1 small onion, roughly chopped
14g root ginger, peeled weight,
    roughly chopped
2 fat garlic cloves, peeled
4 tbsp vegetable oil
2 large-ish tomatoes, quartered
1½ tsp ground coriander
1 rounded tsp ground cumin
¾ tsp garam masala
¼–½ tsp chilli powder, to taste
salt, to taste
large handful of chopped coriander leaves

Cooking canned?

Use 2 x 400g cans, drained and rinsed. You need to help out the flavourings, so add a bit more of everything else. Try 1 medium onion, 4 garlic cloves, 20g root ginger and a little more ground cumin and coriander and garam masala. The method is the same. This version will have a slightly thicker sauce.

A great Goan classic sauce which has a rich tomato flavour rounded off with delicately balanced, spicy, salty, sour and slightly sweet tastes. It works really well with eggs. This dish is very moreish and is one I crave often… eating scrambled or fried eggs no longer has the same appeal. If you are a duck egg fan, this is great with the richer yolks. I like to serve this with rotis or parathas.

Goan egg balchao

Using a stick blender, blend the ginger and garlic with a little water until smooth. Separately blend the tomatoes until smooth. Grind the whole spices and chillies to a powder using a mortar and pestle or a spice grinder.

Heat the oil in a non-stick saucepan. Add the onions and cook over a medium-high heat until well browned on the edges, stirring often. Add the ginger and garlic paste and cook over a medium heat, stirring once the water has evaporated, until the garlic has coloured lightly and the paste has released its oil. Add the tomatoes to the cooked masala with the ground spices, seasoning and sugar and cook over a high heat until it has completely reduced.

Meanwhile, put the eggs on to boil for seven to eight minutes. Take out of the hot water and plunge into cold water to stop the cooking. Once the sauce has reduced, keeping the heat at medium-high, 'brown' the paste until it has darkened considerably, stirring very often. This will really add a lot of depth of flavour.

Once the paste is cooked through, add the vinegar and a good splash of water and simmer until you have a thick sauce. Meanwhile, peel your eggs and halve lengthways. Taste the sauce and adjust the salt, sugar and vinegar, add the eggs and simmer for a few minutes. The sauce should cling to the eggs. Serve hot.

SERVES 4

24g root ginger, peeled weight
10 garlic cloves, peeled
4 large vine tomatoes, quartered
2 tsp cumin seeds
3 tsp mustard seeds
8 cloves
24 black peppercorns
3–5 dried Kashmiri red chillies, whole
6 tbsp vegetable oil
2 onions, chopped
salt, to taste
2²/₃ tsp caster sugar, or to taste
8 large eggs
4 tbsp white wine vinegar, or to taste

This is definitely a special occasion dish, as it is elegant as well as delicious, and worth the effort if you have people coming around. Normally, I stuff the koftas with a spiced mushroom mixture but, as I was writing the recipe, it seemed one step too far and fiddly... so I decided to deconstruct the dish, adding lovely shiitake mushrooms separately, which actually works better. If you want, you can choose to stuff the balls simply with a raisin and a pistachio each. If your paneer is shop-bought, place it in just-boiled water while you work on the sauce, to improve the texture and flavour.

Paneer koftas and shiitake mushroom curry

Soak the cashews in water for 15 minutes, then drain. Blitz to a smooth paste with 1–2 tbsp of water, then set aside. Heat the oil for the sauce in a large non-stick saucepan. Add the black cardamom and onions and cook until well browned. Add the ginger and garlic and cook until lightly colouring. Add the tomatoes, tomato purée, remaining spices and seasoning; cook over a medium heat, stirring, until the water evaporates and the paste releases oil, around 15 minutes. Cook the paste for a few minutes over a moderate to high heat, stirring constantly, to get a better depth of flavour. Add a splash of water, then blend to a purée. Add enough water to reach the consistency of single cream, bring to the boil, cover and simmer for six to seven minutes.

While the curry is cooking, make the koftas. Break up and crumble the paneer until it is fine then, with the heel of your hand, knead until it is even finer (when you squeeze a bit together, it should hold). The more you work it, the smoother it becomes. Add ½ tsp of salt and the coriander leaves and form into large marble-sized balls.

Add enough oil to come 5cm up the sides of a small saucepan and heat to 180°C (350°F). Test the oil by dropping in a small amount of the mixture; it should sizzle immediately but not colour straight away. Add a batch of koftas so that the pan is not over-crowded, then cook, turning halfway, until deep golden. Remove with a slotted spoon and drain on kitchen paper. Repeat with the remaining koftas. Remove most of the remaining oil from the pan, leaving around 1–2 tbsp, then add the mushrooms, season lightly and sauté for four to five minutes.

Once the curry is done, add the cashew nut paste and the cream and bring to a gentle simmer; the consistency should be of a light cream. Add the koftas and mushrooms, return to the boil, then reduce the heat, cover and simmer for five minutes. Taste and adjust the seasoning. Sprinkle over the dried fenugreek and add a swirl of cream and a sprinkling of chopped coriander.

SERVES 5–6

FOR THE SAUCE

50g cashew nuts
8 tbsp vegetable oil
3 black cardamom pods
2 large onions, sliced
25g root ginger, peeled weight, grated
4 fat garlic cloves, peeled and grated
4 large tomatoes, quartered
2 tbsp tomato purée
½–¾ tsp chilli powder
1 rounded tbsp ground coriander
1¾ tsp ground cumin
⅓ tsp turmeric
2 tsp garam masala
salt, to taste
5–6 tbsp double cream, plus more to serve
1 rounded tsp dried fenugreek leaves

FOR THE KOFTAS AND MUSHROOMS

350g paneer (preferably homemade, see page 9)
small handful of chopped coriander leaves, plus more to serve
vegetable oil, to deep-fry
12 shiitake mushrooms, stalks discarded, thickly sliced, or halved if small

The perfect combination of drama, show and pomp. This dish requires a little effort, but all it needs to go with it is a raita and perhaps a salad on the side. I like to use a few different types of mushroom for varying textures and flavours and, if the budget allows, to add a few wild mushrooms. If not, stick to shiitake, oyster and large chestnut mushrooms. The pastry is lovely on top but you can leave it off and finish the dish with the saffron and some roasted cashews instead. The cream and tomato purée are there to balance the flavours of the sauce, so add to taste, and season the sauce well.

Wild mushroom biryani

Start with the mushrooms. Blend together the tomatoes and yogurt until smooth. Heat the oil in a large non-stick saucepan. Add the onions and cook until golden on the edges. Add the ginger and garlic and cook gently until the smell of raw garlic has disappeared, around a minute or so. Add the blended tomatoes, all the spices and the salt and give the pan a stir. Cook this mixture down until it becomes a thick paste and releases oil back into the pan, then continue cooking for another couple of minutes to darken.

Stir in the mushrooms and cook for four to five minutes, or until they release their water (cover the pan after two minutes, but keep giving it a stir). Add 150ml of water and bring to the boil, then simmer for seven to eight minutes or until the whole thing comes together. Add the tomato purée and the cream. Taste and adjust the seasoning, adding more cream or tomato purée to balance the sourness in the tomatoes and yogurt. The sauce should be like thick cream. Take off the heat.

For the rice, heat the oil in a large saucepan. Add the whole spices and cook for 30 seconds. Add the drained rice and stir well. Add 1 litre of boiling water and season generously to taste. Bring to the boil, then cover and cook on a really low heat until the rice is just done, around seven to nine minutes (check after seven). Take off the heat.

Preheat the oven to 220°C/425°F/gas mark 7. Find a suitable dish that is both ovenproof and table ready. Layer half the rice in the dish, then spoon all the mushrooms and sauce evenly over it. Sprinkle over the herbs and finish with the remaining rice. Drizzle over the saffron milky cream. Roll out the pastry on a floured surface to fit the dish, sprinkling with the fenugreek leaves, if using, and a little sea salt, pressing them in so they stay in place. Lift the pastry over the dish, sealing the edges and trimming away excess. Brush with egg, if using. Bake for 30 minutes, or until the pastry is golden and cooked all the way through, then serve.

SERVES 7–8

FOR THE MUSHROOMS

4 large-ish tomatoes, quartered
200g yogurt (if it is quite sour, use just 180g)
5 tbsp vegetable oil
2 onions, finely chopped
25g root ginger, peeled weight, grated
6 large garlic cloves, peeled and grated
1 tsp chilli powder
1½ tsp ground cumin
¾ tsp turmeric
2 tsp garam masala
salt, to taste
800g mixed mushrooms, cleaned and sliced
    or torn into large pieces
1 rounded tbsp tomato purée, or to taste
60ml double cream, or to taste

FOR THE RICE

5 tbsp vegetable oil
2 black cardamom pods
5 each of cloves and green cardamom pods
10cm cinnamon stick
10 black peppercorns
650g basmati rice, well washed, then soaked
    for 20 minutes
small handful of shredded mint leaves
small handful of chopped coriander leaves
good pinch of saffron strands, soaked in
    2 tbsp hot milk and 1 tbsp double cream
    for 30 minutes
250g puff pastry
plain flour, to dust
½ tsp dried fenugreek leaves (optional)
sea salt, to taste
1 egg, beaten (optional)

Beaten rice – poha or powa – is cooked rice that has been flattened into a flake. It is a really interesting ingredient as it is very light and fluffy and has a lovely texture, and you only have to steam it to heat through. This dish is very popular in many parts of India and normally eaten for breakfast. I love it as a light, quick lunch, with a few vegetables. It really is worth seeking out from Indian shops. Don't confuse it with the flaked rice you can find in supermarkets, as that is raw, so cooks differently. This dish would be eaten at breakfast in India, but I mainly make it for a light lunch.

Beaten rice pilaf with peas, potatoes and carrots

Heat the oil in a non-stick saucepan. Add the lentils and cook gently until just colouring. Add the mustard seeds and curry leaves and, once the popping dies down, the onion and green chillies and cook until the onion is just soft. Add the ginger and cook for another minute.

Add the vegetables, salt, turmeric and a small splash of water; give the pan a good stir, bring to the boil, cover and cook for six to seven minutes or until the vegetables are cooked through, checking halfway and giving them a stir.

Quickly wash the rice in some water and add to the pan with another 2 tbsp of water. Cover and steam for three to four minutes, then stir in the lemon juice and check if the flakes are soft. Take off the heat, cover, and leave for another minute. Taste, adjust the seasoning and serve.

SERVES 2, CAN BE DOUBLED

2 tbsp vegetable oil
2 tsp Bengal gram (chana dal), well washed
1 tsp brown mustard seeds
8–10 curry leaves
½ onion, finely chopped
1–2 green chillies, whole but pierced with the tip of a knife
8g root ginger, peeled weight, finely chopped
50g peas
50g potatoes, cut into 2cm pieces
50g cauliflower, cut into 2.5cm florets
30g carrots, cut into 1cm dice
salt, to taste
½ tsp turmeric
150g beaten rice (see recipe introduction)
2½–3½ tsp lemon juice, or to taste

Quinoa needs little introduction these days, it is such a healthy grain that it pops up everywhere. Vegetarians should definitely include it in their diet, as it is high in good-quality protein. This pilaf is a particularly lovely way to cook and eat quinoa. If you don't have ruby chard, use any other leaf in season, from spinach to Savoy cabbage. The cannellini beans add a lovely creaminess, but feel free to substitute any other bean. I find I eat this pilaf as it is and need little else with it, but you can also eat it with a chutney or a raita.

Cannellini bean, ruby chard and quinoa pilaf

Place the quinoa in a saucepan of water, bring to the boil, reduce the heat and simmer until just done, 16–18 minutes for mine (see the packet instructions, but check as it cooks). It will look like it has burst a little. Drain well, then return to the hot pan, off the heat.

Wash, then shred or cut the ruby chard as you prefer. I like to use mostly leaf with just a little stalk, shredded, for colour and texture.

Meanwhile, heat the oil in a non-stick saucepan. Add the cumin and mustard seeds and the dried chilli and cook until the mustard stops popping and the cumin has coloured. Add the onion and cook until soft and colouring at the edges. Stir in the garlic, reduce the heat and cook for a minute. Add the chard, season with salt and give the pot a good stir, then cover and cook over a medium heat until the chard is soft, anything from four to six minutes, stirring occasionally.

Add the beans, some black pepper and the lemon juice and cook until the beans are heated through. Add the drained quinoa and fold through with a fork. Taste, adjust the seasoning and lemon juice, then serve.

SERVES 2, CAN BE DOUBLED

150g quinoa
2 handfuls of ruby chard
3 tbsp vegetable oil
$^2/_3$ tsp cumin seeds
¾ tsp mustard seeds
1 dried red chilli
1 red onion, finely chopped
3 large garlic cloves, peeled and grated
salt, to taste
400g can cannellini beans, drained and rinsed
freshly ground black pepper
2–2½ tsp lemon juice, or to taste

Most recipes on this side of the world that use bulgar wheat are salads, but Indians, particularly the Gujarati people, use it regularly in pilaf. This is a lovely, delicate dish that my mother-in-law first cooked for me after I had my first child: nourishing for a slightly depleted new mum, but light on the system. I so loved the simple flavours and nuttiness of the bulgar that it has remained in my diet; my daughter is now six. Vary the vegetables, using what you have. I eat it with yogurt and a good turn of black pepper. If you won't be eating it with yogurt, add a little lemon juice at the end. I usually cook this just for my little family. You can double the recipe but, if you do, only use 6 cloves and 15 peppercorns.

Vegetable and lentil bulgar

Heat the ghee in a non-stick frying pan. Add the whole spices and cook until the cumin is aromatic. Add the onion and sauté until soft. Add the ginger and garlic and cook gently for one minute, or until the garlic smells cooked and has turned lightly golden.

Add the vegetables, lentils, ground spices, salt and a splash of water. Bring to a boil, stir well, cover and simmer until the vegetables are almost cooked, around five minutes. Uncover the pan to drive off any excess water.

Add the bulgar wheat and stir well. Mix in 300ml of boiling water, cover and cook over a low heat for 13–15 minutes. Check a grain: it should be cooked, if not place back on the heat to steam a little more. Take off the heat but leave to steam, covered, for another five minutes or so. Taste, adjust the seasoning and serve.

SERVES 2–3

1½ tbsp ghee, or a mixture of unsalted butter
  and vegetable oil
5cm cinnamon stick
4 cloves
1 tsp cumin seeds
12 black peppercorns
1 small-ish onion, chopped
12g root ginger, peeled weight, grated
2 garlic cloves, peeled and grated
50g yellow lentils (mung dal), washed well
1 tsp ground coriander
¾ tsp ground cumin
¾ tsp garam masala
salt, to taste
150g bulgar wheat

VEGETABLES I HAVE USED HERE:
6–7 green beans, chopped into 2cm lengths
  (or a handful of peas)
50g cauliflower, cut into 2.5cm florets
50g broccoli, cut into 2.5cm florets
⅓ small red bell pepper, cut into 1.5cm cubes

This is a Tamil dish, made with leftover rice, yogurt and milk. It is delicate in flavour and consistency and perfect for the warmer months, as it is quite refreshing and filling but not heavy. It is lovely as it is, or as a creamy side dish with a vegetable or lentil recipe, or spoon over a little of the Southern Tomato Chutney or Coastal Coconut Chutney (see below and page 19).

Creamy yogurt rice

Bring the rice to the boil in a large pot of water. Simmer for eight or nine minutes, or until soft. Drain, then return the pan to a low flame for two minutes to drive off the moisture. Cover and leave off the heat.

Heat the oil in a small saucepan. Add the mustard and cumin seeds. Once the popping slows down, add the chilli and curry leaves and follow a few seconds later with both types of lentil. Once the larger ones starts to colour, add the ginger and cook for another minute. Pour the whole thing into the pot of rice with the milk, yogurt and salt.

Stir well over a low heat. Taste and adjust the seasoning and yogurt, depending upon how sour it is and how loose you want the consistency. It should be creamy and porridge-like. Serve warm.

SERVES 4–6

175g basmati rice, well washed in several
    changes of water
2 tbsp vegetable oil or ghee
1 tsp mustard seeds
¾ tsp cumin seeds
1 dried red chilli, broken in half
8–10 fresh curry leaves
1 tsp Bengal gram (chana dal), well washed
1 tsp black gram (urad dal), well washed
8g root ginger, peeled weight, finely chopped
250ml whole milk
250–350g yogurt, depending on sourness
salt, to taste

Southern tomato chutney
MAKES 80ML

A lovely spicy, tangy chutney full of the flavours of South India.
  Heat 1 tbsp of vegetable oil in a small non-stick saucepan over a medium heat. Add ½ small onion, sliced, and cook until softening. Add 4g of peeled root ginger and 2 fat, peeled garlic cloves and fry over a gentle flame for one minute. Add 3 small ripe tomatoes, chopped, and salt, cover and cook for five minutes. Blend until smooth, then return to the pan. Heat ¼ tbsp more oil in a separate pan. Add 1 tsp of well washed Bengal gram (chana dal) and cook until starting to colour. Add 2 dried chillies, ½ tsp each of mustard and cumin seeds and a pinch of fenugreek seeds and cook over a gentle heat for 20 seconds, or until the seeds darken. Add 8 curry leaves, give them five seconds, then pour the contents of the pan straight into the chutney. Return the chutney to the heat and add ¼ tsp of tamarind paste, or to taste. Adjust the seasoning and serve.

A biryani is a really special dish from the Moghuls, who made India their home many centuries ago. Originally made with all the ingredients they loved – lamb, rice, saffron, nuts and butter – it now can be made with any ingredient. This version consists of layers of spice-flecked rice hiding a layer of vegetables cooked in a rich sauce. I have departed from tradition and topped it with a layer of delicious fried potatoes and crispy onions. It is a multi-stage dish, but then it is for a special occasion and needs little more than yogurt on the side. (Try it with yogurt into which you have stirred some chopped coriander leaves, shredded mint leaves and seasoning.)

Elegant vegetable biryani

Bring the drained rice and whole spices to the boil in salted water to cover by 3.5–4cm. Simmer for four to six minutes, until just done. Drain the water, return the rice to the heat, allow excess moisture to evaporate for 10 seconds, then set aside. Heat the milk and saffron for assembling the dish together, then set aside.

For the vegetables, heat the oil in a large non-stick saucepan. Add the onion and cook until lightly golden. Add the ginger and garlic and continue cooking until the garlic has turned light golden. Meanwhile, using a stick blender, blend the tomatoes until smooth. Add the spices and tomatoes to the cooked onion, season, then cook down until the tomatoes are getting thick. Add the carrot, cover and cook for five minutes. Stir in the cauliflower, aubergines, mushrooms and yogurt. Bring to the boil, stirring often, then cover and simmer until the vegetables are cooked through, around 10 minutes, adding the peas after five minutes. Add the cream, taste and adjust the seasoning.

Choose a large flameproof and ovenproof dish that has a tight-fitting lid and is table worthy. Butter the base liberally. Spread in half the rice, breaking up any clumps. Season lightly and drizzle over some saffron milk. Spoon over the vegetables, then the remaining rice. Drizzle over the remaining saffron milk, season, then evenly dot cubes of butter on top. Cover.

About 40 minutes before dinner, place the dish in a very large frying pan half-filled with water, to make sure nothing burns. Warm it through for 40–45 minutes, or until you can see the rice steaming inside. (Or cook in an oven preheated to 160°C/325°F/gas mark 3 for 30–40 minutes, or until heated through.)

Meanwhile, deep-fry the sliced onion until deep golden-brown. Remove with a slotted spoon and drain on kitchen paper. Add the potatoes to the oil and fry until golden and cooked; place on kitchen paper and sprinkle with salt and chaat masala. Keep these warm. Just before serving, top the biryani with the potatoes and crisp onions.

SERVES 5–6

FOR THE RICE

450g basmati rice, washed well, then soaked
  for 20–30 minutes
6 cloves
6 green cardamom pods
3 black cardamom pods
2 x 7.5cm cinnamon sticks
2 bay leaves

TO ASSEMBLE

4 tbsp whole milk
large pinch of saffron strands
15–20g unsalted butter
vegetable oil, to deep-fry
1 large onion, sliced
2 potatoes, peeled and thinly sliced
chaat masala (see page 58)

FOR THE VEGETABLES

5 tbsp vegetable oil
1 large onion, finely chopped
35g root ginger, peeled weight, grated
5 fat garlic cloves, peeled and grated
3 tomatoes, quartered
3 tsp ground coriander
1½ tsp ground cumin
2 rounded tsp garam masala
½–1 tsp chilli power, to taste
1 small carrot, peeled and in 1cm slies
300g cauliflower, washed and in 2.5cm florets
4 small Japanese aubergines, in 2.5cm slices
5 large chestnut mushrooms, thickly sliced
140g yogurt
2 handfuls of peas
3 tbsp double cream

This is a really delicious, South Indian-inspired rice dish. The style is typical of the region, with its spicy robust flavours. It is normally made with a coarser, whiter rice of that region, but I use basmati as it is the easiest to find and works well. If you have a hardier rice, now is a good time to use it! This is not supposed to be a fluffy rice dish, in fact it is normally slightly wet and sloppy, but I have made it somewhere in between. It is really moreish and needs little more than some yogurt on the side.

Spiced aubergine and tamarind rice

Wash the rice well in several changes of water and leave to soak in enough water to cover well.

Heat the oil in a large saucepan. Add the mustard seeds and, once the popping dies down, add the curry leaves and the onion; cook until the onion starts to colour on the edges. Add the garlic and cook over a gentle flame for 40 seconds or until the garlic starts to colour. Add the tomato, salt, turmeric and chilli powder with a splash of water and cook over a medium-high flame, stirring often, for four to five minutes.

Drain the rice, then add it and the aubergines to the pan and give them a good stir in the spices. Add 375ml of water, bring to the boil, then cover and cook over a really low flame until the rice has cooked through, around eight to 10 minutes.

As the rice cooks, roast your spices. Heat a frying pan (I use a small cast-iron pancake pan), add the Bengal gram and cook, stirring often, until they turn a lovely golden brown; pour into a spice grinder or mortar. Add the smaller lentils to the pan and repeat until these have gently browned; add to the spice grinder. Add the remaining spices to the pan and roast, shaking, until the cumin and coriander have darkened and are aromatic. Add to the lentils and grind to a powder.

Once the rice has cooked, uncover and add the spice powder and tamarind. Stir well with a fork, adjusting the seasoning as you do. Then cover and leave to steam, off the heat, for a few minutes. Stir in the chopped coriander and sprinkle over the coconut, if using.

SERVES 4

FOR THE RICE
350g basmati rice
6 tbsp vegetable oil
1 tsp mustard seeds
10–12 fresh curry leaves
1 large-ish onion, sliced
2 fat garlic cloves, peeled and chopped
1 large tomato, chopped
salt, to taste
½ tsp turmeric
½–1 tsp chilli powder
36 long Japanese aubergines, cut into
   2–3 pieces depending on length
2 tsp tamarind paste, dissolved in
   4 tbsp boiling water
2 handfuls of chopped coriander leaves
2 handfuls of fresh grated coconut (optional)

FOR THE SPICE BLEND
2 tbsp Bengal gram (chana dal), well washed
1 tbsp black gram (urad dal), well washed
6 green cardamom pods
6 cloves
7cm cinnamon stick
3 tsp coriander seeds
⅔ tsp fenugreek seeds
1½ tsp cumin seeds
12 black peppercorns

Rice is one of the simplest and quickest grains to cook, and good rice is addictive, yet so many people are afraid of cooking it properly. But the technique to cook great fluffy rice is actually really easy. This is how we have always made it in my family; it is foolproof. You can go on to use this simple method to create lovely pilafs.

Perfect boiled rice

Wash the rice really well in several changes of water until the water runs clear. Place in a saucepan and cover with at least 7.5cm of water. Bring to the boil, then reduce the heat to halfway between a simmer and a boil and cook, uncovered, for seven to eight minutes. Try a grain, it should be tender; if not cook for another minute and check again.

Drain, then return the rice to the pan and the heat to dry off any moisture for one or two minutes. Turn off the heat, cover tightly and steam for eight to 10 minutes. Uncover, fluff with a fork and serve.

70–80g good-quality white basmati rice for each person

Everyone needs a pilaf recipe to pull out when you have friends to dinner. This is simple, and you can ring the changes by adding peas or carrots, or fried nuts and raisins for a sweeter version. If you are feeling generous, leave out the turmeric and substitute a good pinch of saffron. It's good with the Royal Raita (see right).

Classic yellow pilaf

Wash the rice in several changes of water until the water runs clear, then leave to soak as you prepare the dish. Heat the oil in a large-ish saucepan. Add the whole spices and fry for 30 seconds. Add the onion and fry until golden.

Add the turmeric and turn in the oil for five seconds. Add the drained rice and stir gently. Pour in 800ml of water, season, bring to the boil and simmer for one minute. Cover tightly and reduce the heat to a minimum. Leave undisturbed. Check after seven minutes; there should be no water left and the rice should be cooked, or nearly so. Cook for another minute or two if necessary. Turn off the heat and leave for five to 10 minutes, then fluff with a fork and serve.

SERVES 4–6

450g basmati rice
4 tbsp vegetable oil
1¾ tsp cumin seeds
3 black cardamom pods
2 x 5cm cassia barks or cinnamon sticks
6 cloves
6 green cardamom pods
1 onion, finely sliced
⅔ tsp turmeric
salt, to taste

This is based on a street food of Mumbai. It is made from cooked rice and vegetables stir-fried with Indian flavourings and a special spice blend on a large, flat, cast-iron pan. It becomes smoky, spicy and tangy. I normally eat brown basmati rice at home, and the nuttiness works really well in this dish. You can add whichever leftover vegetables you have lying around. Here I have kept it simple and made it with just peppers and peas.

Stir-fried leftover spicy tomato and pea rice

Heat the oil in a large frying pan. Add the onion and cook over a high heat until browning at the edges. Add the pepper and chilli and cook for another two or three minutes, or until the onion has well-browned edges. Add the garlic and cook on a low heat for 40 seconds, stirring. Add the tomato, spices and salt and cook over a medium-high heat, mashing the whole thing together, for six to seven minutes.

Add a splash of water from the kettle along with the peas and cook for two or three minutes. Taste to make sure the spices are not raw or powdery and that everything tastes harmonious. Add the rice and stir-fry over a high heat, adding a couple of spoons of water, until the whole thing comes together in a lovely hot mass. Taste, adjust the seasoning and serve with lime or lemon wedges on the side.

SERVES 1, CAN BE DOUBLED

1 tbsp vegetable oil
½ small-ish onion, sliced
½ small red or orange pepper, in 2cm cubes
1 green chilli, whole but pierced with the tip of a knife
2 garlic cloves, peeled and finely chopped
1 tomato, chopped
¾ tsp ground cumin
¼ tsp chilli powder, or to taste
¼ tsp turmeric
¾ tsp ground coriander
½ tsp dried mango powder
½ tsp garam masala
salt, to taste
large handful of frozen peas
200–225g cooked brown basmati rice (around 100g raw brown rice, boiled)
lime or lemon wedges, to serve

Royal raita
SERVES 4

Based on the flavours the Moghuls loved: rose water, fruits and nuts. It's a great, fruity accompaniment to an Indian meal.

Cut a Pink Lady apple into 1cm dice (leave the skin on); you'll need 140g of diced apple. Halve 100g of white grapes, too. Put the apples and grapes in a bowl and mix in 25g each of raisins and pistachios and 300g of yogurt. Now season with ½ tsp of ground cardamom, 2½–3 tsp of caster sugar and up to 1½ tsp of rose essence or rose water. (Be careful with the latter, adding just drops at a time before mixing and tasting, as they can vary in strength.) Serve, sprinkled with more pistachios if you like.

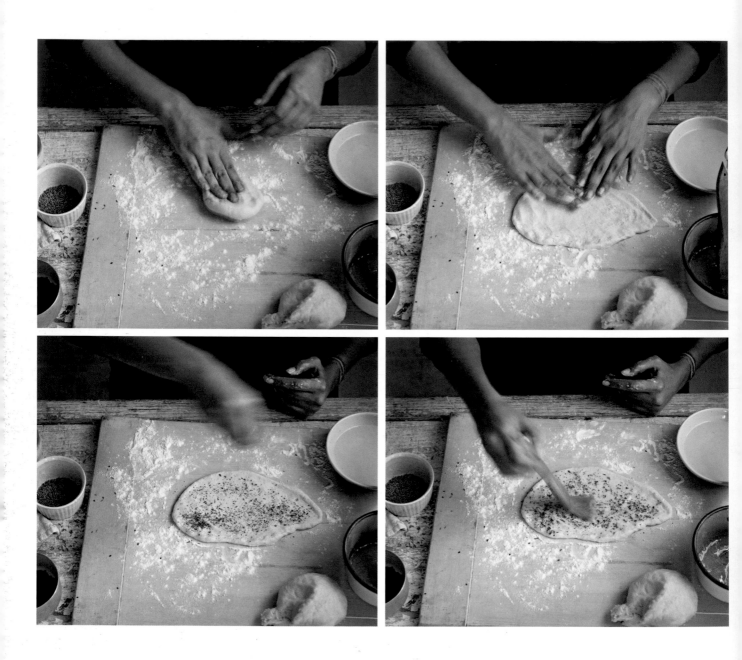

Every time I make naan, I wonder why I don't do so more often. They are so easy and my daughter always comes into the kitchen, bringing her own rolling pin with her. We get stuck in, measuring, kneading, then patiently waiting until we can finish them off; it is lots of fun and good bonding time. This grilled naan is really delicious, crispy on top and soft underneath. I love to top mine with nigella or sesame seeds, or dried mint; my six-year-old daughter stuffs hers with a mound of grated cheddar cheese (see below for her favourite recipe). Stuffing the bread is a great thing to do, and my favourite contains lovely crumbly feta, chopped mint and coriander, finely chopped green chillies and onions.

Best ever grilled naan

Mix the yeast and half the sugar in 4 tbsp of the water. Leave to rest for 10 minutes, or until frothy.

Stir together all the dry ingredients, including the remaining sugar. Make a well in the middle and add all the liquids except the oil. Using a fork, bring the dough together. Take it out of the bowl and knead for six to seven minutes, until soft and smooth (it will be slightly sticky at first). Oil the outside of the dough and place in a large bowl, cover with a tea towel and leave in a warm place for at least two to three hours.

Heat the grill (mine is in my oven) to its highest setting. Place a grill rack or baking tray on the upper shelf. Knock the dough back, flour a work surface and divide the dough into six. It should be very soft. Using a little extra flour, roll or pat each portion into naans that are really thin, ideally less than 1cm thick. (I pat and roll mine into teardrop shapes.) Scatter with the topping, if using, and press lightly in, then brush with some butter.

Place on the hot baking tray or grill rack and grill until the surface has some lovely golden spots, about three to four minutes, then flip and grill for another two minutes or so until the other side has also cooked through. Brush the top side with a little more butter and serve.

MAKES 6 MEDIUM-LARGE NAANS

FOR THE DOUGH
¾ tsp dried yeast
3 tsp caster sugar
130–140ml warm water (different flours will absorb different amounts)
300g plain flour, plus more to dust
scant 1 tsp salt
4 tbsp melted unsalted butter, plus more to grill and to serve
4 tbsp yogurt
a little vegetable oil

TOPPING OR FILLING OPTIONS
nigella, cumin, poppy or sesame seeds, coriander, mint, lightly cooked onions, chillies, grated cheese... or a combination!

Mahi's stuffed grilled naan-wiches

Place a small handful of your favourite hard cheese, grated, in the middle of your rolled-out naan. Bring up the sides and pinch them together like making a bag. Pinch them until they eventually disappear back into the dough. Then flatten with your palms and roll out again. Let mum cook them.

These are the various names for the same basic, everyday wholewheat flatbreads. They are soft and puff up when cooked and, if you have a gas cooker, become a little crisp on the underside. Don't worry about not rolling a perfect circle, practice makes perfect. You can find chapati flour (atta) in most large supermarkets, but if you can't get hold of any, use equal quantities of wholewheat and plain flour. These can be made in advance and reheated, wrapped in foil, in a medium oven. I never put salt in these as they are used to mop up well-seasoned sauces, but others do, so I leave it up to you.

Roti/chapati/phulka

Sift the flour and salt (if using) into a bowl and make a well in the centre. Slowly drizzle in 200–240ml of water and use your hand to draw the flour into the centre, mixing all the time. You may not need all the water as flour absorbs different amounts of water depending on its age and the moisture content in the air. It should be just slightly sticky and will firm up as you knead it.

Knead for eight to 10 minutes, or until the dough seems elastic and most of the joints and lines have worked themselves out. Place in a bowl, cover with a damp tea towel and leave for 30 minutes in a slightly warm area, or at room temperature in the summer.

Divide the dough into 10 equal portions and roll each into golf ball-size balls; cover. Flour your work surface and rolling pin. Roll each ball into a 12.5–15cm circle. The best way is to keep rolling in one direction, turning the dough a quarter of a circle to get a round shape.

Heat a tava, non-stick frying pan or flat (non-ridged) griddle pan until quite hot. Toss the chapati from one hand to the other to remove excess flour, and place on the pan. Reduce the heat to medium and cook until small bubbles appear on the underside, about 10–20 seconds, then turn. Cook this side until it has small dark beige spots.

If you have a gas hob, now place the bread directly over a flame using tongs. It will puff immediately. Leave it for 10 seconds until dark spots appear, then turn and cook on the other side for a few seconds, then remove to a plate. If you have an electric cooker, press down gently on the cooked bread over the hob; as you press one area the rest should puff up. Then tackle the next area. This way the bread should puff up all over. Either way, repeat with the rest of the breads, keeping the cooked breads warm, wrapped in foil, in a low oven.

MAKES 10, CAN BE DOUBLED

300g chapati flour (or half wholewheat and half plain flour), plus more to dust
salt (optional)

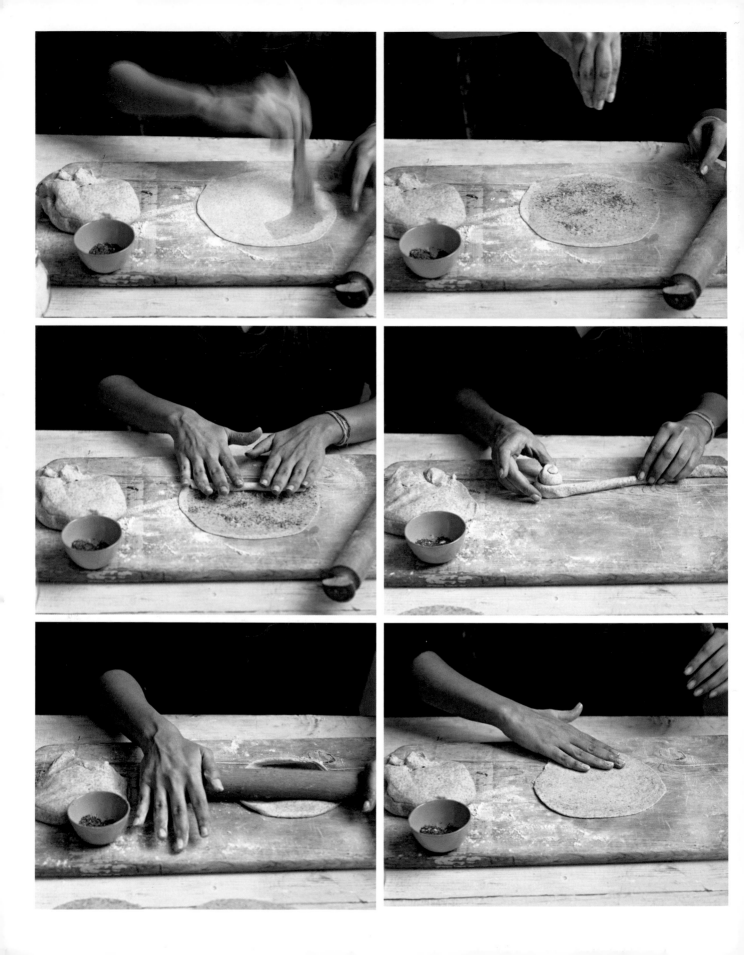

These flatbreads are absolutely delicious, flaky and slightly crisp. They can be plain, cooked with a spice or other flavouring, or even stuffed with a vegetable before cooking. My two favourite types are in the box below right, but you can add anything you like. You can make parathas with vegetable oil, butter or ghee... needless to say, the butter and ghee versions have more flavour, but those made with oil are also delicious. Please note that the parathas in the photograph were made using wholemeal chapati flour, but you can use plain white chapati flour if you prefer.

Paratha, many ways

Mix 200–220ml of water into the flour and knead for eight to 10 minutes, or until the dough seems smooth and elastic and most of the joints and lines have worked themselves out. Make a long log from the dough and divide into 10 balls.

Heat a tava, flat (non-ridged) griddle pan or frying pan. Taking one ball of dough at a time, roll out into a 15cm circle on a floured surface. Brush ¾ tsp of oil, ghee or butter over the surface, sprinkle over a little salt, some flavourings if you want (see below right) and then a fine scattering of flour. Starting with the near edge of the bread, roll away from you into a very tight log (Swiss-roll style). Then using your palms, roll this log a bit longer and thinner. Coil the log in on itself in a tight circular motion and pat down into a thick disc. Flour both sides and roll out into a 15–17.5cm circle again.

Pat off the excess flour and place the paratha on the hot pan, turning the heat to medium-high. Cook until light brown spots appear on the underside, around 10–15 seconds. Turn over and brush ¾ tsp of the oil, butter or ghee over the surface (or do what I do and drizzle it over, then spread with the back of the spoon). Flip the bread again and repeat with more oil. Now, using the edge of the spoon or a knife, make small slashes over the bread to help it crisp up. Turn once again and repeat the slashes. By now the bread should be done, with lovely golden brown spots on both sides. Repeat with the rest and serve hot or at room temperature.

MAKES 10

300g chapati flour (atta), plus more to dust
small bowl of vegetable oil, ghee or melted
  unsalted butter
good pinch of salt

Flavour variations

Spicy: sprinkle a pinch of carom seeds and chilli powder over each bread with the salt, then flour, roll and cook as in the main recipe.

Mint: sprinkle ¾ tsp dried mint (powdered between your fingers) over each bread with the salt, then flour, roll and cook as in the main recipe.

ON THE
SIDE

A restaurant dish and probably a hybrid of some of India's more popular home-grown potato recipes. I have to say this dish beats my own Punjabi cumin potatoes, and it goes with almost everything.

Best ever Bombay potatoes

Bring a large pot of water to the boil and salt it well. Place in the potatoes and boil until just tender (up to 30 minutes). When cool enough to handle, peel and chop into 2.5cm cubes.

Blend together the ginger, garlic and quartered tomato until smooth.

Heat the oil in a large non-stick frying pan. Add the cumin and mustard seeds and, once the cumin starts to darken, add the onion. Cook for a minute before adding the ginger and garlic mixture, the ground spices and salt. Sauté gently for one to two minutes or until the garlic smells cooked. If you are not sure, taste; it should seem harmonious.

Add the tomato wedges, stir well and cook for three to four minutes. Tip in the potatoes and cook for three to five minutes to absorb the flavours. Check the seasoning, stir in the chopped coriander and serve.

SERVES 4-6

salt, to taste
3 large potatoes (around 900g in total), halved
15g root ginger, peeled weight
3 garlic cloves, peeled
2 large-ish tomatoes, one quartered, the other cut into slim wedges
4 tbsp vegetable oil
¾ tsp cumin seeds
1 tsp mustard seeds
1 large onion, roughly chopped
⅔ tsp turmeric
2 tsp ground coriander
1 tsp ground cumin
1 tsp garam masala
½–¾ tsp chilli powder
large handful of chopped coriander leaves

Cauliflower, potatoes and shredded ginger
SERVES 4

A simple dish that is great with a lentil curry. Any leftovers make great panini-like sandwiches, with Tangy Herb Chutney (see page 34).

Heat 4 tbsp of vegetable oil in a large non-stick pan, karahi or wok. Add 1½ tsp of cumin seeds and cook until they are aromatic. Add 2–3 whole, pierced green chillies and 20–25g of julienned root ginger and cook until the ginger starts to colour. Now add 1 tbsp of ground coriander, 1 tsp of ground cumin and ¾ tsp each of turmeric and garam masala with some salt. Cook for one minute. Tip in 400g of cauliflower florets, 250g of peeled potato wedges and a couple of tablespoons of water. Stir well to coat. Cover and cook gently over a medium heat until the vegetables are cooked (around 15 minutes). Stir in 1½ tsp of dried mango powder (which adds wonderful tartness), or 1 small tomato, chopped, and a handful of chopped coriander leaves. Taste, adjust the seasoning and spices, then serve.

If you are a fennel fan, this is a great dish. Panch phoran is a blend of five seeds; if you don't have any you can use a roughly even combination of cumin, mustard, fennel, nigella and fenugreek seeds (though the latter can be left out). This goes well with grilled or tandoori food such as the Tandoori Paneer in my 'PLT' (see page 69).

Five-spiced fennel with tomato

Heat the oil in a non-stick saucepan. Add the panch phoran and chillies; when the seeds stop popping and are aromatic, add the onion. Cook until golden.

Meanwhile, blend together the tomatoes, ginger and garlic with a stick blender until smooth. Add to the browned onions with all the spices and salt. Cook until completely reduced.

Meanwhile, trim off any leafy fronds from the fennel bulb, chop and set aside. Remove any tough or browned external leaves and cut the bulb into wedges through the root. Add the fennel to the reduced sauce with a good splash of water and bring to the boil. Cover and cook until the fennel is tender, around five to seven minutes.

Take off the lid and cook off the excess liquid in the pan; the sauce you end up with should be thick. Taste and adjust the seasoning, sprinkle over the fennel fronds and serve.

SERVES 2, CAN BE DOUBLED

2½ tbsp vegetable oil
¾ tsp panch phoran
1–2 dried red chillies, broken in half
½ onion, sliced
2 large-ish tomatoes
15g root ginger, peeled weight
2 garlic cloves, peeled
1 tsp ground cumin
⅔ tsp garam masala
1½ tsp ground coriander
salt, to taste
1 large fennel bulb, washed

I eat spinach regularly, it seems to go with so many things and is so quick and easy. You can make this with baby spinach or shredded large leaf spinach and leave the leaf whole or semi-blend it, as I do here, which adds a lovely creaminess.

Sautéed spinach, many ways

Heat the oil and butter in a large sauté pan. Add the onion and cook gently until the edges are golden. Add the ginger and garlic and cook until the garlic no longer smells raw, around one minute. Meanwhile, using a stick blender, blend the tomato until smooth. Add the blended tomato, ground coriander and cumin and salt to the pan and cook down until it becomes quite thick, the colour changes and it releases oil back into the pan. Taste; it should seem harmonious. Add the still-wet spinach and allow to wilt down completely.

At this stage, you can go two ways. The first is simplest: taste and adjust the seasoning, adding the black pepper and garam masala with the additional ingredient, if using (I like sweetcorn), and serve. The second way is to remove two-thirds of the mixture, blend it until smooth, then return to the pan. Add the additional ingredient, if using. Taste and adjust the seasoning with the black pepper and garam masala as above. Serve as it is, or with a swirl of single cream.

SERVES 2, CAN BE DOUBLED

1 tbsp vegetable oil
1 tbsp unsalted butter
½ large-ish onion, chopped
6g root ginger, peeled weight, grated
2 fat garlic cloves, peeled and grated
1 ripe tomato, quartered
¾ tsp ground coriander
½ tsp ground cumin
salt, to taste
200g baby spinach, washed well
¼ tsp black pepper
⅓ tsp garam masala
dash of single cream (optional)

OPTIONAL EXTRAS
1½ handfuls of sweetcorn (I use canned)
1 handful of paneer, cubed
1½ handfuls of chickpeas
2 handfuls of sliced mushrooms

Green beans with coconut
SERVES 4

This takes less than 10 minutes to make, and you can use almost any greens: try shaved asparagus or small broccoli florets. You can buy frozen grated coconut in Asian stores, and it's very useful to have in the freezer.

  Heat 2 tbsp of vegetable oil in a large, non-stick frying pan. Add 1 tsp of mustard seeds and, once they pop, reduce the heat and add 8 curry leaves. Once the popping dies down again, add ½ onion, finely chopped, and cook until soft. Add 2 tsp of finely chopped root ginger and 300g of green beans, trimmed and cut into 1cm lengths. Season to taste, add a splash of water and cook over a medium-low flame for around five minutes. Stir in 3 tbsp of grated coconut and 1 tsp of lemon juice, taste, adjust the seasoning and serve.

Inspired by a dish eaten in a friend's house years ago, this was her Hyderabadi mother-in-law's recipe. She served it as part of a meal, but I love it just on its own with crispy naan. Add chickpeas to the spiced oil before tipping it into the yogurt for extra protein, if you want. Pomegranates add a burst of sweet, sour freshness but you can substitute halved baby tomatoes. Lastly, you can griddle the aubergines instead of frying, it will still be lovely.

Crisp aubergines with sweet spiced yogurt and pomegranates

Pour around 1cm of oil in a large frying pan. Add as many aubergine slices as you can get in one layer and cook over a medium-high flame until golden on the base, around two to three minutes. Turn the slices and repeat. Place on two pieces of kitchen paper to drain off the excess oil, then put in a warm oven to keep warm. Repeat with the remaining aubergine. (Alternatively, you can bake the aubergine slices in a preheated oven at 180°C/350°F/gas mark 4, spread out in one layer on a large baking tray, but they will not be as crisp.)

For the topping, heat the oil in a small saucepan. Add the mustard and cumin seeds and, once they start to pop, add the chillies and curry leaves and cook for a further 10 seconds or until cooked through. Pour into the yogurt with the sugar and seasoning.

Place the aubergines on a large serving plate, slightly overlapping in a circular pattern. Spread the yogurt over the central aubergines, leaving a large 7.5cm-ish border. Sprinkle with the pomegranate seeds and chopped coriander and serve immediately.

SERVES 4

FOR THE AUBERGINES
vegetable oil, to fry
2 small-ish aubergines (300–350g each), sliced into 1cm-thick, long slices
good handful of pomegranate seeds
handful of chopped coriander leaves

FOR THE YOGURT TOPPING
1 tbsp vegetable oil
¾ tsp mustard seeds
¾ tsp cumin seeds
2 dried red chillies
12–14 curry leaves
250g Greek yogurt
2 tsp caster sugar, or to taste
salt
freshly ground black pepper

I know many will think life is too short to stuff okra, but this is such an easy recipe and requires very little cooking or chopping. I find I am often drawn to this dish, which I stuff while I am reading something on my computer, or taking a break and watching TV. This is a Gujarati dish, so it is not too spicy and has an element of sweetness.

Coconut–stuffed okra

Mix together all the filling ingredients, adding salt to taste.

Wash the okra and cut a long, deep slit along the length of each finger. Stuff each with as much filling as you can.

Heat the 2 tbsp of oil in a large non-stick frying pan. Add the asafoetida and follow five seconds later with the okra. Give the pan a gentle shake, cover and cook over a medium-low heat until the okra is soft to the tip of a knife, around seven to eight minutes.

Sprinkle over a little sea salt and serve.

SERVES 4

FOR THE FILLING
1 tbsp sesame seeds
1 tbsp grated root ginger
2 tsp ground coriander
1 rounded tsp ground cumin
¼ tsp chilli powder (optional)
¾ tsp garam masala
6 tbsp desiccated coconut
2 rounded tbsp roasted peanuts,
    coarsely crushed
handful of chopped coriander leaves and
    stalks (around 10g)
2 tsp caster sugar
1 tbsp lemon juice
1 tbsp vegetable oil
salt, to taste (ideally sea salt)

FOR THE OKRA
250g okra
2 tbsp vegetable oil
small pinch of asafoetida

Not all lentils have to be cooked to a mush or in a curry. In fact, there are plenty of Indian lentil dishes which are just lightly spiced or flavoured and have no sauce. This easy stir-fry showcases the texture of these great, large yellow lentils. You just need to soak them well in advance, which will really cut the cooking time. These are delicious, really moreish and good with both rice and Indian breads.

Stir-fried Bengal gram with coconut

Heat the oil in a large non-stick frying pan. Add the seeds, chillies and curry leaves. Once the seeds have popped and the cumin has darkened, add the onion. Stir-fry for two to three minutes, then add the garlic. Sauté over a gentle flame until the garlic starts to take colour. Add the turmeric with a small splash of water and cook until the pan is dry.

Drain, add the soaked lentils and salt and give them a little stir in the pan. Add some hot water from the kettle, bring to a boil, and simmer for five to 15 minutes, or until the lentils are tender but still retain their shape. (How long they take depends both on how long they were soaked and how old the lentils are, but they can cook very quickly.) If they are still hard, add a little more water and cook a little longer.

Once they are done, stir in the lemon juice, taste and adjust the seasoning, add the coconut and serve.

SERVES 2–3, CAN BE DOUBLED

3 tbsp vegetable oil
2/3 tsp cumin seeds
1 tsp mustard seeds
1–2 dried red chillies, broken in half
8–10 curry leaves
½ onion, finely chopped
4 garlic cloves, peeled and finely chopped
1/3 tsp turmeric
100g Bengal gram (chana dal), washed well and soaked overnight
salt, to taste
1 tsp lemon juice
4 tbsp grated fresh coconut or 2 rounded tbsp desiccated coconut

---

Spiced sesame seed beetroot with yogurt
SERVES 4

A lovely accompaniment to any barbecue, this is creamy and sweet, with both heat and a lovely nuttiness.

Heat 1 tsp of vegetable oil in a small saucepan, allowing it to pool on one side. Add ½ tsp each of mustard and cumin seeds and, once the spluttering dies down, add to 300g of cooked, cubed beetroot in a large bowl. Add a pinch of chilli powder, 2½ tbsp of toasted sesame seeds, 2 tbsp of shredded mint leaves, 250g of Greek yogurt, a large pinch of caster sugar, and salt to taste. Mix together, adjust the seasoning, and serve.

Cavolo nero, also known as black cabbage, is a much-loved variety of kale from Tuscany. The texture is interesting – less crisp than our familiar cabbages – and the flavour is deeper. I recently rediscovered it at a friend's house. She simply boiled it and, even prepared like that, it stood out. So I bought some and cooked it this way. It has become a staple in my home in the colder months. Buy a head whose leaves are not too large.

Spiced steam-cooked cavolo nero

Prepare the cavolo nero by pulling the leaves off the central core, and cutting out the tough ribs of the outer leaves. The inner, small leaves can be left whole. Wash all the leaves well.

Heat the oil in a large non-stick saucepan. Add the cumin and mustard seeds with the chillies and cook until the cumin has darkened a little. Add the onion and sauté gently until soft. Add the garlic and cook gently until just starting to colour.

Add the cavolo nero and the remaining spices and salt along with a good splash of water and stir to coat well. Cover and steam-cook for four to five minutes, or until the leaves are just soft. Add the tomato and another splash of water if necessary, cover and cook for another one or two minutes, or until it has softened and released some of its juices. Taste, adjust the seasoning and serve.

SERVES 2–3, CAN BE DOUBLED

1 head of cavolo nero
2–2½ tbsp vegetable oil
¾ tsp cumin seeds
¾ tsp mustard seeds
1–2 dried red chillies, halved
½ onion, finely chopped
5 large garlic cloves, peeled and chopped
1 tsp ground coriander
½ tsp garam masala
salt, to taste
1 large-ish tomato, finely chopped
good pinch of freshly ground black pepper

Warm Puy lentils
SERVES 2–3

Earthy but vibrant, I eat these all the time.
Bring 200g of Puy lentils to the boil and cook until just tender, 20–25 minutes. Drain well. Add 1 tbsp of extra virgin olive oil, a fistful of finely chopped coriander, 2½ tsp of roasted ground cumin (see page 9) and 2½ tbsp of lemon juice, season and serve.

Broccoli is one of my favourite green vegetables and often on the menu in my home, although it is not traditionally used in India. This dish is simple but has lovely punchy flavours and is very moreish. Here I like to use small capers in brine as I like the extra tang, but if you use salted capers, make sure you give them a good rinse.

Spiced broccoli with capers

Bring a pot of water to the boil, add the broccoli and return to the boil. Cook for three minutes, then drain.

Heat the oil in a large non-stick frying or sauté pan. Add the panch phoran and chillies and, once they start to colour, add the ginger and garlic, reduce the heat and sauté gently until the garlic is just cooked, around one minute.

Add the broccoli, capers, salt (be careful as the capers are salty) and a very small splash of water and stir until the water evaporates and the broccoli is cooked to your liking. Taste, adjust the seasoning and serve.

SERVES 3–4

450g broccoli, cut into 5cm florets
2½ tbsp vegetable oil
1 tsp panch phoran
1–2 dried red chillies, broken in half
15g root ginger, peeled weight, grated
3 large garlic cloves, peeled and grated
3 rounded tsp small capers (ideally those
   in brine), rinsed
salt, to taste

Ultimate kachumber
SERVES 4–5

A chopped salad served with many Indian meals, this is crunchy, fresh and delicious. It's a case of simply chopping everything finely and mixing it all together. You need 2 large-ish ripe tomatoes, 200g cucumber, 4 radishes, ½ red onion and a large handful of coriander leaves. To this chopped mixture, add 1 tbsp of extra virgin olive oil, 2 tbsp of lemon juice, salt, freshly ground pepper, 1 tsp of roasted ground cumin (see page 9) and 1 tbsp of good-quality dried mint (or fresh shredded mint, if you prefer). Add 1 small green chilli, deseeded and finely chopped, if you'd like more heat. Taste, adjust the seasoning and serve.

DIVINE
DESSERTS

I love dessert and almost need to finish a meal with something sweet. This lovely recipe is inspired by Indian flavours and the country's love of floral notes. It is a soufflé but don't be afraid, it has never failed me and always rises to the occasion with the pomp and gravitas of a presiding maharaja. It might seem like a long recipe of many stages, but it comes together quite easily. I like to eat the dish by making a dent in the middle of the soufflé and pouring in the cream, so every bite is an ethereal mix of cloud-like pomegranate, sweet-sour raspberries, fragrant rose and rich cream. My ramekins hold 150ml; try to stick to that volume, or the cooking times will be affected.

Pomegranate soufflés with rose and raspberry cream

Start with the soufflés. Whisk 25ml of the pomegranate juice into the cornflour. Bring the remaining juice to the boil and reduce to 125ml; it takes around four minutes and you will need to pour it back into the measuring jug to check (don't worry if it slightly over-reduces).

Add the 30g of sugar over the heat and, once it has dissolved, stir the cornflour mixture once more and tip it in (it will thicken almost immediately). Return to the boil, whisking all the while, then boil for 1–1½ minutes. Scrape into a container you can blend in (I use the same measuring jug and my stick blender). Set aside to cool.

Meanwhile, butter the ramekins well and dust with sugar, turning the ramekins so they are well coated and tapping out the excess.

Take 50g of the berries, mash well and push through a nylon sieve. Stir into the cream with the sugar and rose water. Fold in the whole raspberries and adjust the sugar and rose water to taste.

Preheat the oven to 180°C/350°F/gas mark 4. Whisk the egg whites until they reach soft peaks, then sprinkle in the extra 1½ tbsp sugar and continue whisking until the meringue is glossy and firm.

Blend the pomegranate mixture until smooth once more. Place in a large bowl and whisk in around one-quarter of the egg white mix. Then, using a large spoon, carefully fold in the rest, trying to keep the lightness as you incorporate all the little lumps. Do not over-mix. Spoon equally into the ramekins and flatten the tops with a palette knife or other knife. Run the tip of your thumb around the inner rim of the ramekins and place on the middle shelf of the oven.

Bake for eight to nine minutes, or until well-risen and slightly golden on top. Serve immediately with the rose and raspberry cream.

MAKES 4, CAN BE DOUBLED

FOR THE SOUFFLÉS

200ml pure pomegranate juice
2 slightly rounded tsp cornflour
30g caster sugar, plus 1½ tbsp more for the
    meringue, plus more for the ramekins
soft unsalted butter, for the ramekins
2 egg whites

FOR THE ROSE AND RASPBERRY CREAM

150g raspberries
120g double cream
20g caster sugar, or to taste
2 tsp rose water, or to taste

There is an Indian sweet, murabba, which is effectively poached fruit or vegetables in a super-sweet syrup, so they are candied and can be stored for months. This dessert, much loved by my father, always seemed to me to be a waste of good produce, as the end result tastes of sugar and not much else. On the other hand, I love fruits being elevated to pudding status, and poaching a pear is a really elegant and easy way of doing so. The ginger here really complements pears, while the pomegranate seeds help create a dramatic plate and add a lovely astringency and fresh burst of flavour.

Ginger-poached pears with pomegranate and poppy seeds

Place 1 litre of water and the sugar in a saucepan large enough to hold the pears, and bring to the boil, stirring all the time to help the sugar dissolve. Once the sugar has dissolved, add the lime juice and ginger. Peel the pears, then halve, core and slice each half into three wedges. Slip straight into the water. Bring back to the boil, then reduce the heat and simmer gently until the pears yield completely to the point of a knife and appear to be slightly glazed, 18–25 minutes. Using a slotted spoon, remove the pears from the poaching liquor, making sure you leave the ginger in the pot. Reserve the pears. Continue to simmer the liquid for eight to 10 minutes, until it is a light syrup and the ginger looks glazed. Take off the heat; remove and reserve the glazed ginger.

Dry-roast the poppy seeds in a pan (I use a cast-iron one), shaking often for a couple of minutes until aromatic. If using pistachios, dry-roast these until lightly toasted. Whichever you used, remove them from the pan to prevent further cooking.

When ready to serve, pour the pomegranate juice with the 3 tbsp of extra sugar into a pan and bring to a boil. Simmer until the bubbles have enough viscosity to remain on top of the sauce and it has reduced to a thin syrup (it will continue to thicken off the heat).

Meanwhile, divide the slices of pear between four plates, spooning the glazed ginger over. Add a good dollop of cold crème fraîche and drizzle over a little of the hot pomegranate syrup (you will have some left, which is delicious and versatile and can be used for everything from spooning over yogurt to sweetening black tea).

Sprinkle with a pinch of poppy seeds, scatter over some pomegranate seeds and mint leaves and serve.

SERVES 4

100g caster sugar, plus 3 rounded tbsp for the pomegranate syrup
juice of 1 lime
30g root ginger, peeled and coarsely grated
4 firm-but-ripe pears
1 tsp poppy seeds (or 40g pistachios, shelled weight)
600ml pomegranate juice
crème fraîche, to serve
seeds from ½ pomegranate
8 mint leaves

These vivacious little morsels are a perfect combination of sweet, tangy poached dried apricots, cold double cream and delicate pistachios. A deceptively delicious dessert, it is refreshing and satisfying and great as part of a dessert buffet or canapé party. This isn't an Indian dish, but my mother has been making these my whole life and, as they are so easy and delicious, the recipe needed to be shared. Orange blossom is my addition to the dish; it adds another dimension and reflects the Indian love for floral essences but, if you don't have any, just leave it out.

Mum's apricots with orange blossom and pistachios

Bring 700ml of water, the sugar and lemon zest to the boil in a saucepan, stirring all the time to help the sugar dissolve. Add the apricots and return to a simmer. Now cut a circle of greaseproof paper to fit the pan, dampen it under a tap, scrunch it up, then flatten it out and place it in the pan so it rests on the surface of the syrup (this circle of greaseproof paper is called a cartouche). Cook gently until soft but not mushy, 20–30 minutes, depending on how hard the apricots were (mine took 25 minutes). Once soft, remove with a slotted spoon and place on a plate. Leave to cool. Continue to simmer the syrup until it is slightly viscous. Add the orange blossom water, if using. Do not add too much at this stage; you can always add a little more later. Pour into a bowl, cover with cling film and set aside to cool. (You can do this a day in advance.) When completely cold, remove the lemon zest.

Whip the double cream until it holds soft peaks. Create pockets in the apricots by splitting them through their middles, using their natural fold as a guide and making sure both sides are still well attached. Pipe or spoon a generous amount of cream on to the bottom layer, then fold over the top. You should have enough cream in the fruit so that it is well visible. Place on a serving platter, drizzle over the orange blossom syrup and sprinkle generously with the pistachios. Serve.

SERVES 6–8

70g caster sugar
1 large pared strip of unwaxed lemon zest
24 dried apricots (I like large Turkish ones)
½–¾ tsp orange blossom water,
    or to taste (optional)
150ml double cream
good handful of pistachios, roughly chopped

Luscious beetroot halva
SERVES 4

I had never eaten this before makng my own, but I think it is one of the best things you can do with a beetroot!

Coarsely grate 2 large, raw beetroots (wear gloves to keep from staining your hands). Place in a large non-stick saucepan with 1 litre of milk and cook, stirring occasionally, until the milk has dried off; it will take more than an hour. Add 3 tbsp of caster sugar and 4 tbsp of unsalted butter and cook, stirring, for another 15–20 minutes to help the beetroot caramelise. It will turn a lovely, deep colour. Meanwhile, gently heat 1 tsp of unsalted butter and fry 3 tbsp of raisins with a pinch of ground cardamom and a small fistful of cashew nuts until the nuts are lightly golden. Stir into the halva. Taste, adjust the sugar and serve hot.

This is really luscious, billowy yet textured. The custard only takes about 15 minutes to make, but you can buy a 400ml tub of good-quality custard instead (it will have a vanilla flavour, but will be fine). Packets of grated coconut, from the freezer section at Indian and oriental shops, are the best storecupboard cheat and I highly recommend them. You can use desiccated instead, but it will not have the same texture or taste. If you like pomegranate juice, I would add some in as below; it adds a lovely flavour and also soaks slightly into the sponge but, if you don't have any, it still works really well.

Mango, pomegranate, berry and coconut trifle

Start with the custard. Place the milk and cream in a large saucepan and bring to the boil. Meanwhile, whisk the yolks, the 2 tbsp of sugar and the cornflour together in a large bowl until smooth. Slowly pour in the hot cream mixture, whisking all the while so the eggs do not scramble. Pour the whole thing back into the rinsed-out saucepan and place over a gentle heat. Return to just below the boil over a very gentle heat, stirring the mixture constantly; this takes me 10–12 minutes. Cook for another 30–40 seconds, then take off the heat. Stir in the coconut and leave to cool.

Place the strawberries and three-quarters of the pomegranate seeds in a bowl and add the pomegranate juice, if using. Add sugar to taste and a squeeze of lemon juice, to balance the sweet-sharp flavours. Mash some of the strawberries into the sauce and leave to macerate. Meanwhile, prepare the mangoes. Cut the cheeks from the mangoes, peel, then roughly chop. Cut the sides off the stone and see if you can get any unbruised flesh off these as well.

Whip the cream until it is at the soft peak stage.

Cut the cake into 1cm slices and line the base of a glass trifle bowl. Pour over the macerated strawberries and pomegranate with their juices. Spoon the mango evenly over the top. Pour over the custard. Spoon the cream on top, cover with cling film and chill in the fridge until ready to serve, decorated with the reserved pomegranate seeds. You can also use small glasses to make these trifles in individual portions, which look lovely.

SERVES 6

FOR THE COCONUT CUSTARD

200ml whole milk

200ml double cream

4 egg yolks

2 tbsp caster sugar, plus 2 tsp, plus more for the strawberries

1⅓ level tsp cornflour

65g grated fresh coconut (I use frozen and allow it to defrost)

FOR THE REST

175g strawberries, washed, hulled and roughly chopped

seeds from 2 pomegranates

75ml pomegranate juice (optional, see recipe introduction)

lemon juice, to taste

2 large, or 3 medium, ripe mangoes

300ml double cream

275–300g shop-bought madeira cake

This dessert is really special, with the creamy reduced milk, sweet-tart caramelised apple and ricotta. It is simple to make, but you do need to hover around the kitchen as it cooks to ensure the milk does not catch and burn as it reduces. This means stirring the pan, scraping the base with a flat-bottomed spatula, every four to five minutes or so. If you are stepping away from the kitchen, either reduce the heat to its lowest or turn it off until you return. If you prefer you can add 100g of crumbled paneer instead of ricotta. You can make this a day early and chill in the fridge overnight.

Caramelised apple and ricotta kheer

Preheat the oven to 190°C/375°F/gas mark 5. Place the ricotta, slightly spread out in bits, between two layers of greaseproof paper, put it in the oven and bake for 40 minutes. As it bakes it will dry out and become slightly hard. Put a timer on so as not to forget about the ricotta as you reduce the milk. Once done, remove from the oven and leave to cool.

Meanwhile, fill a wide, large pan with enough water to come 5mm up the sides, and bring to the boil. Then add the milk, return to the boil and cook over a low heat, stirring very often and scraping the base of the pan to stop the milk from catching and burning. Cook until reduced by half, it will take 45–50 minutes. (See page 169 for more detailed instructions on how to reduce milk.) Add the rice flour, saffron and cardamom and gently return to the boil while stirring. Cook for another 10–15 minutes, still stirring, adding the 2 tbsp of sugar halfway. The mixture should be one-third of its original volume. Remove from the heat.

Towards the end of the cooking, peel the apples and grate on the coarse side of a box grater into long strands (I grate them straight into a non-stick pan). Place on the heat and add the butter and the extra 2 tsp of sugar. Sauté over a moderate flame until the apple has turned a lovely pale gold and is slightly caramelised, around three minutes. Take off the heat.

Once the milk, apples and ricotta have cooled, mix together, taste and adjust the sugar if necessary, adding more milk if the kheer seems too thick. I like mine lightly creamy, but everyone likes it slightly differently.

Pour into a serving dish and chill in the fridge. Sprinkle with the flaked almonds to serve.

SERVES 6

200g ricotta
1.5 litres whole milk, plus more if needed
1 tbsp rice flour
pinch of saffron strands
¼ tsp ground cardamom
2 tbsp caster sugar, plus 2 tsp, or to taste
2 firm, sweet-tart apples (I use Pink Lady)
1 rounded tbsp unsalted butter
flaked almonds, to garnish

Hot sticky pineapple, crisp pancakes, cold cream and a hint of spice. Lovely. These are inspired by a very typical Indian dessert pancake, made in the cold months, that is deep-fried, then glazed in a sugar syrup and eaten with sweetened thickened milk. This is my quicker and easier version and works beautifully. Unfortunately the pancakes cannot be made in advance, but they don't take long to cook (the batter can be ready to go) and it all comes together quite quickly.

Sticky caramelised star anise pineapple on crispy pancakes

Place the sugar in a large frying pan and allow to melt and caramelise until golden. Add 4 tbsp of boiling water; it will bubble and seize but keep stirring and the caramel will melt back in. Add the pineapple and star anise and cook over a moderate flame, turning the pineapple in the caramel often and moving around the pan if there are obvious hot spots. Once the fruit is lightly golden and glazed, which takes four to five minutes, add two small knobs of butter and shake them in. You can add a spoon of hot water at any time if the caramel looks like it is becoming too dark. Keep cooking the pineapple, turning in the sticky caramel, until the rings have a lovely golden colour and are well glazed. Set aside. These can be made in advance and reheated when you are ready to eat; I add the extra knob of butter as I do so.

Make the pancakes. Mix together the flour, sugar, cardamom, salt and ground almonds. Add the butter and milk and whisk until homogeneous; it should have the consistency of thick cream.

Heat half the ghee in a large non-stick frying pan until quite hot and drop around 1½–2 tbsp of batter in for each pancake. You should be able to make three at a time, each about 10cm in diameter (help them spread with a spoon). Reduce the heat to medium-low and cook until golden on both sides and slightly darker at the edges, a matter of one or two minutes each side. Lift out with a slotted spatula and place on kitchen paper to drain any excess ghee. Repeat with the second batch.

Place a pancake on each plate and cover with the shards of pineapple. Top with a spoon of crème fraîche and a star anise from the pan and sprinkle over the toasted coconut. Serve immediately, drizzling with any of the pineappley, caramelly juices from the pan.

ENOUGH FOR 6, CAN BE DOUBLED

FOR THE PINEAPPLE
3 tbsp caster sugar
4 x 1cm pineapple rings, skin, eyes and core removed (I sometimes slice these in half, and a bit of imperfection is good here)
6 star anise
2–3 small knobs of unsalted butter
150g crème fraîche
3 tbsp desiccated coconut, lightly toasted until golden

FOR THE CRISPY PANCAKES
70g plain flour, sifted
55g caster sugar
1 brown cardamom pod, seeds pounded in a mortar and pestle (or a pinch of ground cardamom)
pinch of salt
2 tbsp ground almonds
30g unsalted butter, melted
100–120ml whole milk
4 tbsp ghee or vegetable oil, for frying

Kulfi is India's national ice cream. It is often served with a mass of clear cornflour noodles doused in rose syrup. You cannot buy those noodles here, but you can buy very fine pre-roasted vermicelli from Indian shops and I think it's better than the original! I have also discovered violet syrup (I get mine, the Présent brand, online); it has all the floral notes of rose but is more delicate and has fast become a staple in my house (my daughter even drizzles it over pancakes). The entire combination is divine: hot delicate vermicelli, cold creamy kulfi, the slight bite of nuts, all rounded off with a lovely finishing note of violets. I often make a double batch of kulfi in two large saucepans, so I can save some for later.

Cardamom kulfi with violet-laced vermicelli

Bring the milk to the boil in a heavy-based pan over a moderate flame, stirring often. You need to make sure it doesn't boil over or burn. Stay close to the pan and stir, scraping the base so the milk does not catch, stirring the skin that forms on the surface back in and scraping down the sides of the pan; these bits are all an integral part of the kulfi. Simmer over a medium heat and reduce until just 600–650ml remains; it will have turned a light cream colour. The whole thing will take around 1½–2 hours over a medium heat, so be prepared and make it at a time when you need to be in the kitchen anyway. It's worth the effort, as a kulfi which is not properly reduced will be icy rather than creamy.

Add most of the sugar and all the ground cardamom, return to the boil and cook for a few minutes more. Add the cream, then taste and adjust the sugar, bearing in mind that as it freezes the sweetness will dull a little. Leave to cool, then add the pistachios and almonds.

Pour into your moulds (I use 150ml pudding basins and cover with cling film). Once the mixture is cold, place in the freezer; they will take around five to six hours to freeze. Stir once or twice as they are freezing, to redistribute the nuts.

About eight minutes before you want to serve, take out the kulfis. Place a pot of water to boil on the hob. Break the vermicelli and drop large strands into the boiling water on the hob, then boil for one minute. Take one out, it should be soft; if it is, drain all the noodles.

Two to three minutes before serving, place the kulfi moulds, open side up, in a deep bowl of just-boiled water to help liquify the edges, making sure the water does not get in the moulds. Invert the kulfis on to your serving plates and place a moat of vermicelli around them. Drizzle the syrup over the vermicelli, sprinkle over the chia seeds, if using, and the extra nuts. Add some edible flowers if you can find them, and serve.

MAKES 4, CAN BE DOUBLED
(BUT IF YOU DO, USE 2 PANS OR IT WILL TAKE MUCH LONGER)

1.5 litres whole milk
3–4 tbsp caster sugar, to taste (I add the smaller amount)
½ tsp ground cardamom, or to taste
6 tbsp single cream
1 rounded tbsp pistachios, sliced, plus more to serve
1 rounded tbsp almonds, sliced, plus more to serve
60–80g roasted very fine vermicelli (see recipe introduction. I would make extra, but then I think I am greedy here!)
around 2 tbsp violet syrup
1 tbsp chia seeds, to serve (optional)
fresh edible violets, to serve (optional)

I was at first very sceptical at how an egg-free cake would taste and, more importantly, how the texture would be. This recipe was given to me by a friend of mine, Divya, about three years ago. I have to say it was a revelation. It has a lovely texture and crumb and the cake is light and rises really well. The orange syrup adds a lovely sour, sticky note and the dates a great chewy texture, propelling this simple cake into an elegant, impressive dessert. The cakes can be made a day in advance, they won't be hot but they will still be delicious. You can also make one large cake; just make sure it is cooked all the way through by testing with a toothpick.

Fluffy egg-free pistachio cakes with orange syrup and dates

Preheat the oven to 190°C/375°F/gas mark 5. Line the base of eight 150–200ml pudding moulds (mine are metal) with greaseproof paper and butter the sides well.

Beat together the condensed milk and butter until well blended and creamy. Stir in 240ml of water, add all the remaining ingredients and stir well to mix.

Spoon evenly into the moulds; the mixture will be thick. Place in the middle of the oven and bake for 25 minutes, or until a toothpick inserted into the middle comes out clean.

Meanwhile, pour the orange juice and zest and the sugar into a small saucepan and bring to a boil. Simmer until, when you drop a bit on a cold plate, it feels slightly syrupy to the touch. It will continue to thicken further as it cools.

Place a cake on a plate and spoon over some orange syrup. Place the date slices on the syrup and spoon a generous dollop of the crème fraîche on the side, or on top. Scatter over a few pistachios and serve.

MAKES 8

FOR THE CAKE

150g unsalted butter, at room temperature, plus more for the moulds
360–370ml (440-450g) condensed milk
150g pistachios, ground to a coarse powder
260g plain flour, sifted
1 tsp baking powder
1 tsp bicarbonate of soda
pinch of salt

TO FINISH

juice of 2 large organic oranges and finely grated zest of 1
6 tbsp caster sugar
8 large unsweetened dates, sliced
crème fraîche, to serve
handful of chopped pistachios, to serve

ACKNOWLEDGEMENTS

The first vegetarian influence in my life was my mother, and her simple but delicious take on vegetables cast a positive glow on vegetarian food in my early years. But a proper induction came with the large, extended Jain / vegetarian family into which I married. It was really a case of you marry me, you marry my family and all that comes with it! In particular I'd like to thank my mother-in-law who, from the very beginning, has openly and passionately shared her knowledge of Indian vegetarian dishes and made sure, throughout the last decade or so, that I try as many delicacies and interesting flavour combinations as she has. Some people say that vegetarians know little about good food; nothing could be further from the truth. My new family are veggie food snobs and seek and expect the best flavours from every meal.

A massive thanks to Heather Holden-Brown and Elly James for their honest and sound guidance; Anne Furniss for green-lighting this book and for her continued support; the team at Quadrille for the much necessary behind-the-scenes work; Lucy Bannell for being as 'geeky' about words as I am about food; Claire Peters, Emma Lee, Joss Herd and Tabatha Hawkins for making the food and book come to glorious, colourful and appetising life.

I would also like to thank my family for their continued support as I juggle work and children and, lastly, thank you Shaila for taking the time, as always, to be my sounding board, and whose critical eye and frank comments I have come to rely upon to make sure the book is as good as it can be.

EDITORIAL DIRECTOR Anne Furniss
CREATIVE DIRECTOR Helen Lewis
PROJECT EDITOR Lucy Bannell
DESIGNER Claire Peters
PHOTOGRAPHER Emma Lee
FOOD STYLIST Joss Herd
PROPS STYLIST Tabitha Hawkins
HAIR & MAKE-UP Madge Foster
PRODUCTION DIRECTOR Vincent Smith
PRODUCTION CONTROLLER James Finan

First published in 2012 by
Quadrille Publishing Limited
Alhambra House
27-31 Charing Cross Road
London WC2H 0LS
www.quadrille.co.uk

Text © 2012 Anjum Anand
Photographs © 2012 Emma Lee
Design and layout © 2012
Quadrille Publishing Limited

The rights of the author have been asserted.
All rights reserved. No part of this book may
be reproduced, stored in a retrieval system
or transmitted in any form or by any means,
electronic, electrostatic, magnetic tape, mechanical,
photocopying, recording or otherwise, without the
prior permission in writing of the publisher.

Cataloguing in Publication Data: a catalogue record
for this book is available from the British Library.

ISBN 978 184949 120 4
Printed in China